T0205181

"The joy of the series, of reading *Remote Control*, *Golf Ball*, *Driver's License*, *Drone*, *Silence*, *Glass*, *Refrigerator*, *Hotel*, and *Waste* . . . in quick succession, lies in encountering the various turns through which each of their authors has been put by his or her object . . . The object predominates, sits squarely center stage, directs the action. The object decides the genre, the chronology, and the limits of the study. Accordingly, the author has to take her cue from the *thing* she chose or that chose her. The result is a wonderfully uneven series of books, each one a *thing* unto itself."

Julian Yates, *Los Angeles Review of Books*

"The Object Lessons series has a beautifully simple premise. Each book or essay centers on a specific object. This can be mundane or unexpected, humorous or politically timely. Whatever the subject, these descriptions reveal the rich worlds hidden under the surface of things."

Christine Ro, *Book Riot*

". . . a sensibility somewhere between Roland Barthes and Wes Anderson."

Simon Reynolds, author of *Retromania: Pop Culture's Addiction to Its Own Past*

OBJECT LESSONS

A book series about the hidden lives of ordinary things.

Series Editors:

Ian Bogost and Christopher Schaberg

Advisory Board:

Sara Ahmed, Jane Bennett, Jeffrey Jerome Cohen, Johanna Drucker, Raiford Guins, Graham Harman, renée hoogland, Pam Houston, Eileen Joy, Douglas Kahn, Daniel Miller, Esther Milne, Timothy Morton, Kathleen Stewart, Nigel Thrift, Rob Walker, Michele White.

In association with

BOOKS IN THE SERIES

email

From: RANDY MALAMUD
<rmalamud@gsu.edu>

BLOOMSBURY ACADEMIC
NEW YORK • LONDON • OXFORD • NEW DELHI • SYDNEY

BLOOMSBURY ACADEMIC
Bloomsbury Publishing Inc
1385 Broadway, New York, NY 10018, USA
50 Bedford Square, London, WC1B 3DP, UK

BLOOMSBURY, BLOOMSBURY ACADEMIC and the Diana logo are
trademarks of Bloomsbury Publishing Plc

First published in the United States of America 2020

Cover design: Alice Marwick

Bloomsbury Publishing Inc does not have any control over, or responsibility for,
any third-party websites referred to or in this book. All internet addresses
given in this book were correct at the time of going to press. The author and publisher
regret any inconvenience caused if addresses have changed or
sites have ceased to exist, but can accept no responsibility for any such changes.

Library of Congress Cataloging-in-Publication Data
Names: Malamud, Randy, 1962- author.
Title: Email / Randy Malamud.
Description: New York, NY : Bloomsbury Academic, 2019. |
Series: Object lessons | Includes bibliographical references and index.
Identifiers: LCCN 2019011527 (print) | LCCN 2019012868 (ebook) |
ISBN 9781501341915 (ePub) | ISBN 9781501341922 (ePDF) |
ISBN 9781501341908 (pbk. : alk. paper) Subjects: LCSH: Electronic
mail messages. Classification: LCC HE7551 (ebook) |
LCC HE7551 .M35 2019 (print) | DDC 004.692–dc23
LC record available at https://lccn.loc.gov/2019011527.

ISBN: PB: 978-1-5013-4190-8
ePDF: 978-1-5013-4192-2
eBook: 978-1-5013-4191-5

Series: Object Lessons

Typeset by Deanta Global Publishing Services, Chennai, India
Printed and bound in the United States of America

To find out more about our authors and books visit www.bloomsbury.com
and sign up for our newsletters.

CONTENTS

PART ONE

PREMAIL

*Thinking about its simplicity, we can persuade ourselves
that we know everything that we need to know
about e-mail.[1] It is, apparently, merely letter writing
by a different means. Thinking about e-mail as an
infinitely complicated gestalt, however, we can easily
conclude that it has overtaken us without our really
understanding what it is.*

PHILIP STEVICK, "THE INNER LIFE OF E-MAIL"[2]

"What hath God wrought" was, famously, the world's first
telegraph message: arguably, even, the first email, depending
on what email means. The aptly awesome biblical quotation
(Numbers 23:23) traveled the wires on May 24, 1844, from
the U.S. Capitol, where Samuel F. B. Morse had set up his

contraption, to a Baltimore railroad station where his colleague, Alfred Vail, stood by to receive and decode the ciphers that were embossed into a thin paper strip. Some claim Vail actually invented "Morse Code," the electromagnetical dot-and-dash pulses (not unlike today's 0/1 binary digital signals) that propelled the words, letter by letter, from sender to recipient.

Certainly, Morse's dispatch was an impressive debut for the medium, but I am more bemused by Vail's response.

He wrote back to Morse: "What hath God wrought."

Granted, Vail had obviously never received such a message before, but still, he failed spectacularly to maximize the power of telecommunication.

He should have said something else.

Taking Morse's cue, he might have volleyed back with a biblical reference of his own. "O Lord, how manifold are thy works!" from Psalm 104 would have been an inspired choice: "In wisdom hast thou made them all: the earth is full of thy riches."

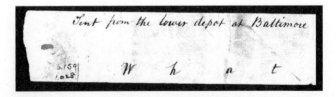

FIGURE 1 Say what: In the first telegraph message, a letter-by-letter transcription appears beneath each mechanical impression of the dot-and-dash code. Smithsonian National Museum of American History.

Even a polite banality would have served: "Yes, indeed," while forgettable, would have been a legitimate *response*.

Or, had Vail imagined how the miraculous speed and reach of the new medium buzzing at his fingertips would empower human communication and displace the supremacy of the Divine Word, he might have deconstructively lampooned Morse's theology: "Thus spake Zarathustra" would have been enormously clever. He would have had to delay his response for forty years to send that message, as Nietzsche wasn't born until five months after that first telegraphic communiqué was sent, but just imagine: if Vail had transmitted that pearl of wisdom, we might celebrate him instead of Morse today as the man who prophetically anticipated where all this electrical chatter was headed. "What hath God wrought?" "God is dead!" That would have been a comeback for the ages, an email that mattered.

(Perhaps, in his defense, Vail foresaw that a return email includes the original text: "each message contained the one that had come before, so your own words came back to you," as Elif Batuman explains.[3])

Prompted by Morse, Vail finally began to participate in a back-and-forth that approximates contemporary email patter. Morse asked his associate to carry on a conversation for the amusement of the audience in attendance: "Stop a few minutes," said Morse. "Yes," Vail answered.

"Have you any news?" "No." "Mr. Seaton's respects to you." "My respects to him." "What is your time?" "Nine o'clock, twenty-eight minutes." "What weather have you?"

"Cloudy." "Separate your words more." "Oil your clock-work." "Buchanan stock said to be rising." "I have a great crowd at my window." "Van Buren cannon in front, with a fox-tail on it."[4]

Overcoming his initial echolalia, Vail got the hang of it, chatting with his correspondent about the weather and political news. Some of their messages—"Oil your clock-work," "Separate your words more"—remind me of email exchanges I have with my sons: "Turn off autocorrect," they instruct; "Activate wifi."

Is it surprising that after Morse asks if there is any news and Vail replies "No," the exchange continues for eleven more messages?

A decade after Morse's triumph, Henry David Thoreau muses: "We are in great haste to construct a magnetic telegraph from Maine to Texas; but Maine and Texas, it may be, have nothing important to communicate."[5]

Today, when we log on to the most incredible communication network that humanity has ever created and send forth our interminable missives, are we doing any better than Morse and Vail did in their debut? Are we actually saying anything worth saying? Or are we just blathering—gigabyte upon gigabyte of sound and fury, signifying nothing?

How did we get here? Some time in the 1990s we began, with some trepidation as I recall, to enroll for a service (AOL? HoTMaiL? Yahoo?) that promised to connect us, electronically and efficiently, to our friends and lovers, our bosses and merchants. It seemed a bit skeevy (there was a whiff of porn and lewd chatrooms associated with it); superfluous (we were doing just fine interacting with each other via available technologies); juvenile and undignified (like two kids with a tin-can phone connecting their bedroom windows, or passing notes in class, or sharing secrets that nobody else cared about on squawky walkie-talkies).

There was a small subscription cost at first, but soon it became free. (Is it really free? It is *perceived* to be. . . .) If it initially seemed that the nature of our correspondence was changing simply in scale—our mail would be faster, cheaper, more easily distributed to large groups—we now realize that email entails a more fundamental alteration in our consciousness. "Light is shot directly into our eyes," John Freeman writes, capturing the neurobiological intensity and intimacy of email. "It is beamed right into our pupils."[6]

What can we do about it? How can we separate the wheat from the chaff? Can we seize control, rather than allowing the tail to wag the dog? The younger generation seems to be giving up on email entirely, turning instead to a media array that grown-ups don't even know how to use. Do such platforms as FB, IG, Snapchat, Twitter, and IM come under the heading of "email," I wonder? There is terminological bleed: "let me check my email" might mean consulting Google, a smartphone app, GPS, text messages, Wikipedia, anything else on the Internet, a fitness watch, or any other object that's generally digital and communicative.

Everything is email, always already. All these technologies are more similar than different in terms of their discourse, their immediacy, and their ubiquity; logging into one of them seems to log us in to all of them. The category of "social media" may not technically include email, or at least pretends not to. Social media's mission is, in fact, precisely to compensate for the perception that email is an 800-pound gorilla, a ratty dotard babbling to himself off in the next room, stumbling through the digital revolution with fusty content that is overwhelming, banal, random, antisocial. Trendy and innovative, social media offer a zippy, schticky, new and improved version of the OG . . . though destined to become exactly what they are trying to displace. Mel Brooks warns: "We mock the thing we are to be."[7]

So for better or worse, even as newer variants render it passé, email is here to stay and we would be smart to figure out how to revivify it (assuming it ever had any vitality in the first place). Applying my conventional English-professor skills to an unconventional textual genre, I will examine how the discourse of email both extends and disrupts established traditions of letters, writing, rhetoric, and social communication. Though email may seem inherently devoid of literary or aesthetic significance, do not be surprised if I find a bit anyway: my guild is pretty good at ferreting out scraps of cultural meaning and interest, diamonds in the rough, however grim the pickings may appear.

The first bona fide email message is lost to posterity. Ray Tomlinson—who may or may not have been email's "Morse";

Shiva Ayyadurai, too, stakes a (tenuous) claim—says he can't remember the first email he sent, or the exact date he sent it. The transmission occurred on a U.S. Department of Defense network called ARPANET some time in 1971. "Most likely the first message was 'QWERTYUIOP' or something similar," Tomlinson guesses.[8] Or it may have been "TESTING 1 2 3 4."[9] "The first e-mail is completely forgettable," he told an interviewer, "and therefore, forgotten."[10] Tomlinson sent the email to himself, thus obviating the need for a response and avoiding a potential "Vail fail." (I email myself all the time: sending myself reminders, transferring files from my home computer to my work computer, or forwarding myself something from the depths of my inbox so it rises to the top. If I haven't received an email in an hour or two from someone else, I send myself one to make sure it's still working. Even if you could email things only to yourself, this would still be a pretty impressive technology.)

Perhaps email would be less existentially confounding if it were more concretely objectful. I miss letters. No splitting hairs here—letters were wonderfully, incontrovertibly resplendent as objects. Virginia Woolf agrees with me:

When the post knocks and the letter comes always the miracle seems repeated—speech attempted. Venerable are letters, infinitely brave, forlorn, and lost. Life would split asunder without them. "Come to tea, come to dinner, what's the truth of the story? have you heard the news?

life in the capital is gay; the Russian dancers. . . . " These are our stays and props. These lace our days together and make of life a perfect globe.[11]

An email is like a letter shorn of almost everything people liked about letters. It is, perhaps, a "condensed letter" or an "essence of letter." An email is just words: packaged together with codes, commands, formats, and attachments, but fundamentally, words—electrified

YES OR NO

FIGURE 2 "Yes or No." Charles Dana Gibson, *Collier's Weekly*, 1905. Minneapolis College of Art and Design Library, CC BY 2.0.

words moving very fast, liberated from the albatross of paper, ink, envelopes, seals, grand neoclassical edifices for sorting, liveries and vehicles for delivery, and all the other spectacular inefficiencies endemic to a letter's objectness. Letters moved through the world quite speedily, all things considered, but email moves so much faster because it jettisoned archaic deadweight. The feel and smell of stationery, the confident authority of the letterhead, the art of penmanship and especially the closing signature in the writer's hand, the tidy archivability of the document . . . all are now dismissed as superfluous. I don't have space to write a whole eulogy for stamps but, please, just *remember stamps*! They were incredible too.

"The last letter will appear in our lifetime," Simon Garfield predicts (though he also concedes that Queen Victoria complains in her correspondence, "Nobody writes letters nowadays" and "The art of letter writing is dead").[12]

There will never be an email equivalent of Martin Luther King Jr.'s, "Letter from Birmingham Jail," or Elizabeth Bishop and Robert Lowell's literary correspondence, or Eleanor Roosevelt and Lorena Hickok's epistolary passion. An exception that proves the rule is Kathy Acker and McKenzie Wark's flirty, gossipy email exchange, *I'm Very into You*,[13] a delightful voyeuristic spectacle, though loosey-goosey in a way that a vintage epistolary correspondence wouldn't be. Like Renzo Piano's Centre Pompidou in Paris, it's the lone postmodern iteration of a type that exists so there don't have to be any more of them.

Émile Zola's *"J'Accuse!"* was a letter—an open letter—*au Président de la République*. Is there such a genre as an "open email"? The only thing that comes to mind is accidentally hitting reply-all.

Think of the commercial value letters held: a letter (unsent) written from the *Titanic* the day before it sank sold for six figures: "This boat is giant in size and fitted up like a palatial hotel. If all goes well we will arrive in New York Wednesday AM."[14] President Lincoln's letter responding to a petition from children asking him to free the slaves brought $3.4 million at auction; he wrote, "Please tell these little people I am very glad their young hearts are so full of just and generous sympathy . . . and that, while I have not the power to grant all they ask, I trust they will remember that God has, and that, as it seems, He wills to do it."[15] (Lincoln loved telegraphs too: he spent hours in the War Department's Telegraph Office, sometimes even sleeping there, reading frontline dispatches and sending commands back to his officers.[16])

Letters had narrative value: think of Edgar Allan Poe's purloined letter, Pamela's letters to her parents. They had spiritual value (Screwtape's letters, the Pauline epistles to the Corinthians, Romans, Galatians, Hebrews). They had erotic value (Fanny Hill's letters to Madam; the obviously spurious but nonetheless arousing letters to *Penthouse*). Letters had political value: Alexander Hamilton's correspondence to his lover, Maria Reynolds, ended up (thanks to James Monroe) in the hands of his adversary Thomas Jefferson; Hamilton's presidential aspirations were shattered after he threw himself on the public's mercy by publishing the letters himself.[17]

Letters embodied the values of our imaginations: "I am 8 years old. Some of my little friends say there is no Santa Claus. Papa says, 'If you see it in *The Sun*, it's so.' Please tell me the truth, is there a Santa Claus?"[18] They had social value: literacy rates jumped globally in tandem with the invention and expansion of mail service.

There will never be a valuable email, a famous email, a celebrated email. There will never really be an important email. Even in 2016, when a U.S. presidential election turned on a collection of home-brew email, tens of thousands from Hillary Clinton's ignominious private server, and another WikiLeaked batch from her campaign chair John Podesta, what were they about? In one, senior Clinton Foundation official Peter Huffman writes:

```
Question: why do I use a 1/4 or 1/2 cup of
stock at a time? Why can't you just add 1 or 2
cups of stock at a time b/c the arborio rice
will eventually absorb it anyway, right?
```

Podesta responds (with no time to edit, possibly because he is so busy losing an election):

```
Yes it with absorb the liquid, but no that's
not what you want to do. The slower add
process and stirring causes the rice to
```

```
give up it's starch which gives the risotto
it's creamy consistency. You won't get that
if you dump all that liquid all at once.[19]
```

I concede that email is ultimately, if just tenuously, an object. It's a paltry and often disappointing object, a grammatically challenged object, a shape-shifting object. It's an object ricocheting through cyberspace in search of validation; it don't get no respect.

It's surprising how pedestrian email is, how banal, given how intricately interwoven it is with our existence. Or maybe it's not surprising at all: maybe it's just the mirror held up to life, and we are precisely as trite as our email suggests.

'Twas ever thus: "there is no standard nowadays of elegant letter writing, as there used to be in our time. It is a sort of go as you please development, and the result is atrocious."[20] This complaint was prompted not by email but by the growing fad of postcards (popularized for Americans at Chicago's 1893 Columbian Exposition, after Europeans had embraced the craze a few years earlier) which threatened to destroy the eloquent epistolary tradition, some feared. Short, informal, and comprised of dubiously grammatical prose, postcards were a corrupting influence on civil society. Sound familiar? Email is the most loathsome, artificial, degrading, reductive communication technology ever invented . . . except for all the others.

In nineteenth-century Russia they wrote letters, as Dave Malloy's postmodern musical send-up of *War and Peace* explains. The song "Letters" extols the value and joy of epistolary communication: "We put down in writing what is happening in our minds." Once it's on the paper, they feel better, because "It's like some kind of clarity when the letter's done and signed."[21]

These letters embodied and conveyed their correspondents' ideas, their intelligence, their emotions, their values. And the act of composing and sending these letters, Malloy hazards, made the writers feel better; it produced clarity. Lives were lived, assignations were arranged, manifestoes were mailed, wars were waged. People communicated and society flourished as writers committed words to paper, and other writers responded with other words on other paper.

PART TWO

EMAIL

E-mail is a medium through which professional stress can reach workers who no longer feel protected by the traditional barriers of place and time.
FERNANDO LAGRAÑA, *E-MAIL AND BEHAVIORAL CHANGES*[1]

If e-mail could speak, what would it say?
JONI TURVILLE, "INTERVIEWING OBJECTS IN A DIGITAL WORLD"[2]

1 OPEN

The individual email is a unitary, bounded collection of codes and data, one item in a much larger system also, in the aggregate, called email, produced by a technology commonly known as email, which uses the medium of email to email an email. (I cannot resist: "The medium is the message.") Email is many things, many related but distinct operations and significations. But is it an actual object? Rarely, one might print out an email on paper, which may seem to embody email-as-object. But email is not meant for reading on paper. "Please consider the environment before printing," email signatures commonly hector. "Don't waste resources." "More than half of all pages printed are never used." To print is to misconstrue, even to desecrate, its ephemerally luminous quality.

I am not suggesting that email is completely, innately objectless: indeed, that would invalidate the discourse, the trope—the object!—you now hold in your hand. A book titled *Email* in a series called Object Lessons would seem to demonstrate unequivocally that email is an object.

But email is a paradoxical object consisting in some part, even in *considerable* part, of objectlessness: of that which it is not. An iteration of something (now obsolete) that once resembled it, it is mail, but it is also not mail. It is elusive, insubstantial. There are so many emails that they may be invisible. They are so necessary that they are worthless; the idea of email is so brilliant that it is inane.

Email may point to a concrete object, or emanate from such an object, as you find when you search your account for a keyword that will yield your hotel address, the technician's time of arrival, or instructions on how to return a bum purchase. The Radisson, your oven, and an unappealing towel (that looked more sumptuously absorptive online than it turned out to be irl) are objects that have been ensconced in email, facilitated by email, so there is a second-degree objectness here, consequent upon its service as conveyor or conduit of objects. Email may be an object by association, by implication, by extrapolation. "Viaduct" might be a better category than "object" to classify email: certainly a viaduct can also be an object, but such an object is more fundamentally about moving, processing, transmitting, and sorting other (more material) objects that pass through it. "Email is really nothing more than a medium," Merlin Mann says. "It gets things from one place to another."[1]

Jobs and relationships begin and end on email. Births and deaths make inboxes chime with the same tone as a missive about a late Nigerian prince whose estate inexplicably wants to send me $6.2 million. The things that flow through this conduit are polyvalent and polymorphous. We might characterize the object as news, or stuff, or desire, or disappointment: an object fabricated with abstraction, metaphysicality, that challenges us to describe, to quantify, to hold and feel, and collect and appraise it *qua* object.

FYI: It is probably not the case that contemporary society is doomed to falter in an anarchic miasma merely because the triumph of email has left us in a post-epistolary funk. Still, I cannot resist putting forth that possibility as the end point of a continuum on which we appraise the *quidditas*, the essence, of this relatively recent and unbelievably ubiquitous phenomenon. "A letter, by its inherent nature, indicates thought," writes Stanley Solomon. "E-mail is inherently anti-contemplative."[2]

Not just letters have been superannuated, but even conversation itself: speech was "the mode in which most relationships have traditionally been conducted," but email "is increasingly normalized as a mode of social interaction" in commercial, professional, educational, and personal communication.[3] Hamlet's dying words, "The rest is silence," would make a great email signature sign-off.

We spend our days writing, reading, sending and resending an enormous corpus of tediously insipid texts. People who once wrote perhaps a couple of letters a day might now send a dozen emails in an hour. "How we spend our days is, of course, how we spend our lives," Annie Dillard observes. "What we do with this hour, and that one, is what we are doing."[4]

Mahatma Gandhi warns: "No man can be turned into a permanent machine."[5]

I will presume agreement on the premise that in the age of email, compared to any preceding era, the quantity of written correspondence is up and quality is down. As we slog through the collective consciousness of our grotesquely overstuffed inboxes, we can fine-tune this initial analysis to determine what email means, what is missing, what is new, and ultimately, at the end of the day, how we might do better. How could we try to attain a higher caliber of performance with this medium—smarter content; more thoughtful interaction; less mechanical and more humanistic in sensibility, affect, voice; less confusing, sloppy, and random (which is to say, *more effectively communicative*) in terms of tone, style, lingo; better liked and valued by its practitioners?

What, in a nutshell, are the rules of email? What is its mission statement? Apparently nobody really knows . . . not even me. Email is quick and convenient, its admirers proclaim: it "can get anyone's attention at the fucking speed of light," says CEO Stewart Butterfield.[6] Is that enough? McDonald's is quick and convenient, as are cigarettes, Uber, and Internet porn. Not exercising is quick and convenient, as are not reading and not voting. The point being: just because something is quick and convenient does not mean that it improves our lives or adds to the splendor of our civilization. Fast is great, sometimes, but the speed of modern existence has sparked a resistance, a rebuttal, in the form of the slow food movement, slow TV, slow fashion, slow living, and so on. And slow on.

Individual email habits are idiosyncratic—ways of organizing the to's and from's, styles of responding, formal informalities, varieties of signatures, methods of archiving, ways of ensuring that responses and action items have been processed. (Nearly every email I have received from my friend S.—who has published six books with Cambridge University Press—has been composed between 6:45 a.m. and 7:00 a.m. These are not unrelated data points.)

Most people seem to have a philosophy of email, though usually, they tell me, it is not one that they had bothered to articulate until I asked them. They have principles about how email should convey a certain standard of professionalism and proper social etiquette: what styles and voices best suit email exchanges with family, friends, students, bosses, business contacts. Most people feel confident that their own email demeanor is sensible and appropriate, while everyone else is too sloppy or too stiffly formal, too longwinded or too elliptical, too fast or too slow.

We can begin to anatomize the vacuity of email by noting the dearth of expressive terminology to describe its process and product. Think of the resplendent prEmail epistolary vocabulary for texts and technologies: missives, love letters, poison pen letters, fan letters, chain letters, Dear John letters,

letters of introduction, letters of apology, condolence cards, get well soon. There are men of letters (who may have started out as letter boys), Colleges of Letters, and Republics of Letters. There are letter-openers and envelope-sealers, letter trays, letter scales, letterheads, letter carriers, letterweights, letter racks. W. H. Auden delivers a splendid array of letters in "Night Mail":

> Letters of thanks, letters from banks,
> Letters of joy from girl and boy,
> Receipted bills and invitations
> To inspect new stock or to visit relations,
> And applications for situations,
> And timid lovers' declarations,
> And gossip, gossip from all the nations,
> News circumstantial, news financial,
> Letters with holiday snaps to enlarge in,
> Letters with faces scrawled on the margin,
> Letters from uncles, cousins, and aunts,
> Letters to Scotland from the South of France,
> Letters of condolence to Highlands and Lowlands
> Written on paper of every hue,
> The pink, the violet, the white and the blue.[7]

An autodidact was called "letter-learned": someone who advanced herself by reading letters, writing letters, and just generally living in, and soaking up, the richly stimulating milieu that was the world of letters. Deleuze and Guattari might say she was *becoming* lettered. "Letters" was a synecdoche for the study and mastery of written texts (philosophical, literary, and scholarly, among others). "By letters and by science is the man made semblable or lyke to god" wrote William Caxton in 1483.[8]

Try to imagine describing a comparable character today, self-taught and self-improved, as "email-learned." LOL! WTF?

Envision a cabinet of wonders filled with all the fascinating ephemera that has been superseded by email. Email needs no racks or scales, no weights or openers, and that freedom from cognate tools and *objects* works to its detriment: people liked twiddling with gizmos and contraptions. OMG, think of postboxes of different lands: English red pillar boxes, U.S. "snorkel" collection boxes for drive-through deposits, funky modern Dutch orange boxes, Deutsche Post *Briefkasten* featuring a stylized post horn, the brass instrument that signaled the mail coach's arrival. Mailboxes are vanishing, redundant, poof, in the age of email. (You could think of your computer terminal as a pomo mailbox, but really, nobody does.) A few rusting holdouts still stand sadly in public places: convenient places to hide bombs during parades, they'll be collector's items in a decade.

Lacking all these accoutrements, what vocabulary do we have today to describe and accessorize our email communication? There's "phishing," which is not too bad—it's a "sensational spelling" (deliberately incorrect for effect: for example, Krispy Kreme, Mortal Kombat) with an etymological nod to "phreaks," telephone-era hackers, and also referencing a fishlike HTML tag used in chat transcripts about how to commit web fraud.

"Spam" is clever, from Monty Python's famously ironic paean:

Spam! Spam! Spam! Spam!
Spam! Spam! Spam! Spam!
Lovely spam! wonderful spam![9]

"Tubes" is good too, also ironic in its mockery of the late Alaska senator and amateur Internet theorist Ted Stevens, who explained,

The Internet is not something that you just dump something on. It's not a big truck. It's a series of tubes. And if you don't understand, those tubes can be filled and if they are filled, when you put your message in, it gets in line and it's going to be delayed by anyone that puts into that tube enormous amounts of material.

(In the same Senate hearing where he explained how the tubes work, Stevens also referred to an email message as "an Internet," bless his heart.)[10]

But *spam*, *phishing*, and *tubes* are outliers. Mostly, the language of email involves off-putting technical terms and imponderable acronyms, way too many acronyms: HTML, IMAP, MIME, LAN, TCP/IP, DNS, FTP, nodes, servers, clients, headers, domains, timestamps, data, data, data, .com,

THE INTERNET
A series of tubes.

FIGURE 3 In homage to Sen. Ted Stevens. Knowyourmeme. com. CC BY-NC-SA.

.gov, .edu. When email's rampant popularity meant that it needed to get faster and providers broadened the bandwidth data transmission, what did they call this next-generation upgrade? Broadband. (-, -) . . . zzzZZZ. They should've consulted the French engineers who named their new fast trains TGV, *très grande vitesse*! You can't say "tay jhay vay" without feeling a rush of speed; you can't say "broadband" without feeling like an IT geek.

It's all strikingly graceless and user-unfriendly, hindering our embrace of the technology we use so heavily. We feel at sea, most of us, because we can't understand and don't like the argot. When we talk about what we're doing on email, we don't feel snazzy; we sound clunky. In the world of XML, ASCII and routers, we don't really know what route we're on, which makes us feel like anxious, tentative bystanders. Stepping onto the TGV, I feel like I'm going very fast before the train even leaves the station; talking about email, I sound like a confused poseur, out of my depths. (A great grab-quote for a viciously negative review of this book: "a confused poseur, out of his depths.") Even the *Oxford English Dictionary*, a dependably gushing stream of etymological fascination, has little luster in its definition of email: "A system for sending textual messages (with or without attached files) to one or more recipients via a computer network (esp. the Internet); a message or messages sent using this system."

"Email" is unexciting in other tongues too. It is one of those terms that most languages don't even bother trying to translate. The fanatically francophone Académie Française tried to mandate *courriel* (from *courrier electronique*, electronic mail)—but it didn't take. In Yiddish—yes, Yiddish has taken the trouble to coin a word—*blitzpost* is not too bad ("*blitz*" = "lightning").

A Google image search for "email" generates a visual portfolio as bland as the linguistic one (see Fig. 4).

I suggest that this descriptive and semiotic dullness indicates a larger impoverishment. My hope is to enliven the medium, the artifact, the act of email—which I plan to do by poking it with a stick until it turns up something interesting.

FIGURE 4 Email, iconographically. Google and the Google logo are registered trademarks of Google LLC, used with permission.

Back in 1844 when Morse was getting this all under way, skeptics of the new electric technology derided it as quackery resembling mesmerism, hypnotism, or some other brand of "Black Magic."[11] Some thought his technology would be able to cross boundaries between not merely Maryland and the District of Columbia but also between life and death: people "believed such missives could be transmitted not just across great distances, but to and from the great beyond."[12] Spiritualism was the thing of the moment, and the incredible new phenomenon of *electricity* buttressed the claims of those who believed that invisible forces might facilitate communication to invisible realms, such as the afterlife. (Even today, an app called Phoenix—get it?—allows users to get the last word by sending email posthumously.[13])

We remain enthralled by the electric e: Where can we not go, what can we not see, under the enchanted ether of e?

E for everybody. Email: mail plus e. And/or, mail by e. A subset of mail, a genre of mail, denoted by e; inflected by e. The e stands for electronic, though this etymological resonance is increasingly attenuated, like the x in X-ray (so called because its essential nature was unknown at the time) or the g in G-string (origin indeterminate). After all, everything is now electronic—e might as well stand for *everything* as much as it stands for *electronic*. E equals energy. Einstein, himself an E, must have thought he had pretty much cornered the market on e back in 1905 with his theory of special relativity; mass—energy equivalence: $E = mc^2$.

But no one could have predicted what the modern age had in store for the letter e.

Silent e? Not any more: e has a lot to say! It is, beyond dispute, the letter of our times. E always had it good. It is the most commonly used letter in English: 12.7 percent of all letters are e. It comes from the Semitic letter *hê* (their fifth letter, as it is ours), which may have started as a praying or calling human figure (*hillul*: rejoice, jubilation), probably based on an Egyptian hieroglyph.

A similar Siniatic symbol, the right-hand figure in the Wadi el-Hol inscription, shows a man praying. Tip him sideways, lose his head and other extraneous body parts, and voila, he becomes the letter E.[14]

A28

FIGURE 5 Pre-e. Gardiner's sign A28. Nilemuse.com, GNU Free Documentation License.

FIGURE 6 The Wadi el-Hol inscription, Egypt, c. 2000 BCE, depicts the ancestor of E (far right). Drawing by Marilyn Lundberg, West Semitic Research. Wikimedia Commons.

I sometimes reprise, myself, this ancient expressivist letter-pose. I enact this ancestor of e, this prototype of e, this dance of e, in moments of both success and failure, connection and misconnection: expostulating with the brio of my own Semitic jubilation when I have found a strong wifi network; or, less salubriously, waving my device around in the (delusionsal?) belief that if my signal is spotty, I may still manage to "catch" a small piece of Internet as I flail, and may thereby connect to e(mail).

E is in the throes of a millennia-long journey, a symbolic journey, a linguistic journey, a journey of ideas and of spirituality, of evolution, enunciation, emotion, elaboration. The *pièce de résistance* of this ubiquitous letter, the *ne plus ultra,* lies in the ubiquity of email. If we think of a letter in search of an object, email embodies e's exultance in this enterprise. There are other objects, too, affixed to e: e-cigarettes, e-books, e-content, e-waste. In Scientology, an E-meter measures electrical changes in the body to determine a person's mental state. In a rave, e is ecstasy, a psychoactive drug that dissolves fear and relieves tension. But it is email that has become the pitch pipe we use to determine the key of E, where "on forever's very now we stand" (in the words of, obviously, E. E. Cummings).[15]

Speaking of overdetermined email signifiers, where did @ come from? Who would've guessed that it would be the dingbat of the future? If you had registered a © for @ thirty years ago, you would be a wealthy person today. Generally (awkwardly) called "the at sign," there is no specific English word for it. The French call it *arobase*, and other languages have colorful nicknames: in Israel it's a "strudel," in Croatia a "monkey," in Danish an "elephant's trunk," and in Mandarin Chinese it's a "little mouse."

Email engineer Ray Tomlinson—who signs his name "R@y" when giving autographs[16]—used the @ sign to distinguish emails arriving from remote computers,

so the format was "Tomlinson@remotemachine" (the .com and the like would be invented later). The choice was happenstance: as Tomlinson later told the Smithsonian, he'd been looking around for something to use when he noticed the @, poised above "P" on his Model 33 teletype terminal. "I was mostly looking for a symbol that wasn't used much . . . I could have used an equal sign, but that wouldn't have made much sense." That the @ key was even on the computer keyboard was itself rather by happenstance, too. Its origins are obscure (one theory suggests it is an "a" placed within an "e" and an abbreviation for "each at"); it was sometimes used in commerce to designate the price at which each unit was being sold.[17]

A rotund and cozy symbol, @ has been inducted into MoMA's architecture and design collection. "Conceptually, what @ has done is signify the internet as a destination: the @ symbol is 'at,' therefore the internet is a place one can go."[18]

But is it though? Where exactly would we go, to go to the Internet? For a few years, and this was sort of fun, we hung out in Internet cafés, especially when we were traveling—but in most of the world those have gone the way of Blockbuster Videos, telephone booths, and Western Union.

We say we're *on the Internet* rather than *at the Internet*: suggesting that it is, somehow, a platform, a foundation, a surface of some sort—with a network of tubes running beneath, obviously; possibly pneumatic? I feel certain that Sen. Stevens imagined them to be pneumatic tubes, like those used by the nineteenth-century New York City postal system that could propel a canister from the Eighth Avenue General Post Office to Grand Central Station in four minutes.

"On the Internet" is like "on the phone"—*on* means "using," as in "on the road": taking advantage of the public highways; "on the air": making use of a technical communication network. The user may be literally "on" something—as when we're on the road—or "on it" in the sense that "it" (the phone, the radio, the Internet) is *turned on* (working, powered up, accessible) and the user is utilizing this on-ness.

"On" bespeaks a figurative locationality: a person who's "on the wagon" or "on the ball" or "on the button" isn't really on a wagon, ball, or button. In the early days of telephone service, "on the phone" meant "connected to the telephone network": someone asking if you were "on the phone" wanted to know whether or not your home had a phone. The same usage recurred when email arrived and some people had it but more people didn't. "Are you on email?" meant "Do you have email?" or "Can I send you an email?"— followed, if the answer was affirmative, by exchange of email addresses. I remember the first time anyone gave me an email address—it was my Israeli cousin, Benush—and he ended it with "dotcom." I asked him a few times to repeat himself;

I didn't understand what that meant, and he just repeated, increasingly annoyed, "dotcom." He has a thick accent, so I wrote down something like "dakkam"; I figured it out a few months later when I was given my second email address.

I remember being a bit hesitant to go on email in those days (c. 1991) for a few reasons: it seemed as if we might be getting in over our heads, technologically; it seemed pointless; it seemed likely to make us vulnerable to who-knows-what might come through the tubes. We were managing swimmingly with letters, phone calls, and interoffice memos (and also faxes—which were initially called "electronic mail," btw[19]), so why rock the boat? Being on email seemed somehow beneath me, as a professor: it had a louche air.

I do not recall having any earthly idea what sorts of things would actually be communicated via email—one more reason I was in no hurry to sign up. I finally joined the club at the moment when about half my colleagues, all the younger ones, had signed up for it, and seemed to be sending (sometimes) interesting things to each other. The other half, my elders, seemed as if they would never sign up for it. (In the end, maybe half of that cohort grudgingly did, and half didn't: for a long time those last holdouts would ask office staff to send and receive email on their behalf. We mocked their disconnectedness, but also, after a while, we envied their . . . disconnectedness.) Eventually a notice from our provost informed us that henceforward we were considered responsible for reading and acting upon any email sent to us by any office in the university. There was no going back from that. The notice was sent by email, which seems like a logical glitch: preaching to the converted.

I digress: I was at @. PrEmail, "at" made perfect literal sense as a preposition to associate with an address or phone number: those digits and words indicated, simply, where the desired recipient was. A telegraph, letter, summons, postcard, or phone call was directed to a place designated by a certain precise and unique arrangement of figures so that it would be *at* that place where the intended recipient, too, was *at*. Mobile phones began to disrupt this locational precision, and then email piled on the wagon (not actually "on" any actual wagon: a figure of speech!) by disentangling where you were at (where you lived, or worked, or vacationed) from where your email would go. One facet of cutting-edge new media/GIS retained (and even hyperprivileged) actual at-ness, and that is, of course, GPS. You were exactly *there* . . . no, now *there*! I mean, *there,* right there! GPS took up all the at-ness; cornering the market, it left everything and everyone else free to wander at will. At least a certain amount of locational value was lost: for example, answering the phone no longer served as an alibi that you were at home studying as you were supposed to be. (Disable the GPS tracker!) But much more was gained in terms of safety and emergency preparedness, flexibility for last-minute changing plans of meeting places, @hither instead of @yon, and the ability to talk with people while you were on the bus, at the park, in the restaurant: anytime, anywhere.

So, I revisit the premise that "the @ symbol is 'at,' therefore the Internet is a place one can go." Different users may experience different levels of comfortable orientation and geolocation (at different times) while they are *on email*, or perhaps in some sense *at email*. Ze may feel that ze knows where ze is (e.g., on email on hir computer at work in the field) to a degree that satisfies hir sense of place and stability; ze may have a clear, untroubled vision of the boundaries and the relational proximity, the terrain on which ze might map hir email connections and correspondences, hir subjects, forwards, and replies-all, hir audience, hir community.

And this community may even be supermobile, hyperglobal in its reach. Email allows relations to be "established and maintained across vast distances without requiring any participant to stir out of her or his present location," writes Emma Rooksby; it "permits meetings of distant minds and engagement in cross-cultural exploration," and may facilitate "'world-travelling,' exploring the lived worlds of others in ways that transform their understanding of their own self and culture."[20]

But on the other hand—and I think many of us may be *on* this hand—we may feel anxiously free-floating and dislocated the more time we spend on email. The fantasy of empowering and unfettered locational ubiquity may be counterposed by the reality of anomic, disorienting confusion, and dislocationality. "Everywhere" may finally be not that different from "nowhere." Emailers may feel uncertain whether they are *at* home or *at* work, since they may be working on work-email at home and vice versa. They may be abroad but still emailing as if they were in their native environs. They may have a sense of where their correspondent is emailing from, or they may not. That correspondent may be a relative, friend, neighbor, or colleague; or she may be a stranger they will never meet.

The sharper sense we once had of where our correspondents were located is now more obscure. As long as we know where they are @, we don't need to know where they are at: "@" is not so much a synonym for "at" as it is a replacement, a displacement, of at. It is a disparagement of "at," even a postmodernist ironic deconstruction: *the end of at*. Having broken down barriers and boundaries, email is by definition free-range: un- or even anti-geographical. The infinitude of virtual space, for better and worse, supplants literal space, personal space. Object lesson: people who spend a great deal of time on email may lose sight of where they (and others) are at. This might be worth worrying about.

As long as we're microscoping "e" and "@," we might take a quick scan of "mail" as well. (And why not the erstwhile hyphen too? Sure—I'll get to that in a minute—) Here is "mail" in its first occurrence, thirteenth century: "A bag, pack, or wallet; a travelling bag." Then, four centuries later, "A bag or packet of letters or dispatches for conveyance by post (more fully *mail of letters*). In later use chiefly: the postal matter (or a quantity of letters, packages, etc.) conveyed in this manner; all that is conveyed by post."[21]

The thing that carried it came first, etymologically, and evolved into the thing that is carried. With computers, too: people invented the conveyer, and then created something

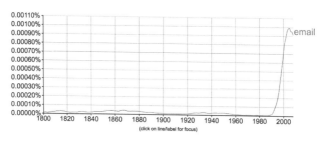

FIGURE 7 The rise of email. Google Books Ngram Viewer.

to convey therein. A "mail of letters"—exquisite. Shortened, because life is too short: now just "mail."

Linguistically, Google's big data corpus, Ngram, illustrates email's recent skyrocketing popularity (see Fig. 7).

The slight downturn in the early twenty-first century correlates with when my students, and my sons, stopped returning my email. Those tiny blips occurring from 1800 to 1990 are either optical character recognition (OCR) mistakes for words like "small" or "entail" misread by Google's scanning technology, or iterations of the French or German word "enamel"—*émail* and *emaille*, respectively: a delicately exquisite and untroubled medium completely unrelated to email except through a quirk of coincidental translational orthography, and whose object-hood it would be much more straightforward to interrogate. If this book were about *émail* (*cloisonné* beads, porcelain bowls, *en résille* crystal, Fabergé eggs), the object lesson might be, simply, "beauty is truth, truth beauty." Or, alternatively—considering the profusion of *émail* found in the post-revolutionary ruins of aristocratic estates—"If you can keep your head when all about you are losing theirs. . . . "

Last but not least, the hyphen: style manuals differ, but they generally used to recommend "e-mail," and have been shifting over the past few years to the sleeker and slightly shorter "email." (The *New Yorker* retains "e-mail," and, I imagine, always will. They also use "reëlect," "naïve," and "preëminent," God love them.) "Newly coined nonce words of English are often spelled with a hyphen," Donald Knuth writes, "but the hyphen disappears when the words become widely used" (as "non-zero" and "soft-ware" have become "nonzero" and "software"). "Thus it's high time for everybody to stop using the archaic spelling 'e-mail.' Think of how many keystrokes you will save in your lifetime if you stop now!"[22]

Visually, I think, "e-mail" did a better job of identifying the two different media, the two concepts, that combine in this hybrid object; though certainly, one might argue conversely, that the combination is clearer, tighter, more linguistically seamless, with the single-word portmanteau, sans punctuation. As in H-bomb, A-frame, T-bone, T-shirt, and X-ray, the orthographic impact of "e-mail" preserves a sense of an original object, bomb/frame/bone/shirt/ray/mail, that is significantly but efficiently (using only one letter!) transformed into something cognate but distinctly unique. There's no confusing an H-bomb with a regular old bomb, or a G-spot with any other corporeal area. We wouldn't write Hbomb, Dday, Tbone, or Gspot because they would look odd: the spelling wouldn't give good visual guidance about pronunciation. "Email" strikes my eye, at first glance, as resembling "Emily," and suggests that the first syllable might be "em" (with a short *e*) rather than "e" (with a long *e*). I don't think "e-commerce" or "e-learning" will evolve into "ecommerce" or "elearning": they simply look too weird. "Etailing" and "ecruiting" are trying to become words (describing online retail business and hiring); I strongly suggest we don't let them in.

Usage habits, which probably offer the best guidance, are clearly trending toward the minimalist camp of "email." In a Twitter poll[23] my editor posted to curtail my dithering, 80 percent thought I should 86 the hyphen and so it shall be.

2 PASSWORD

Passwords are for secrecy; breached passwords entail exposure. A Russian crime ring stole 1.2 billion passwords in 2014. North Korea's "Lazarus Group" hacked into Sony's email that same year, leading to a slew of revelations about celebrities' medical conditions, salaries, diva personalities, and executives' racist musings about whether President Obama liked movies with black casts. A 2013 Yahoo hack by "state-sponsored agents" affected all three billion of their customers, they admitted four years later (after having initially given lower figures). "Onliner," a spambot, harvested over 700 million email addresses and passwords in 2017. River City Media, another spam operation, was found in 2017 to have infiltrated 1.3 billion email accounts.

Such large-scale hacks harvest and monetize information that allows criminal access to bank accounts, tax records, credit cards, cloud services, and other vulnerable data. (Who among us does not recycle the same password for some—all?—of these accounts? I have even heard it rumored that some people have an email folder titled "password" in which they store all their log-ins and passwords to all their accounts.) The thieves may break into our various accounts themselves, or they may outsource part of their crime by selling the information to others. As humdrum as our email may seem to us, it can be a treasure chest for hackers. More focused attacks on individual email accounts may be designed to blackmail someone or discover personal secrets. Celebrities are especially vulnerable to such hacks: David Beckham, Sarah Palin, Paris Hilton, and Colin Powell have all been embarrassed by material discovered in their email. Discrediting climate science was the motive for hacking staff email accounts at the University of East Anglia's Climate Research Unit.

Security experts suggest we might protect ourselves from rampant hackery by creating an anagram from a sentence "using symbols and numbers to make it more complicated. For example, the sentence 'One time in class I ate some glue' could become 1TiC!AsG."[1] It makes me want to throw up my hands in resignation and change all my passwords back to "password."

Someday, computer innovators predict, passwords may be replaced by optical recognition or a system that detects each person's unique pattern of touch on the keyboard. Let's hope that happens sooner rather than later, but in the meantime, I'm afraid, the bad guys have won. There is simply no way that we can keep in our heads the new and improved super-safe passwords that would provide immunity from identity thieves. The cognitive pathways by which people perceive, process, understand, and remember words prevent us from being able to embrace such random strings of characters as "1TiC!AsG."

In cartoons from the olden days, a character might spout an obscenity that would be censored and rendered as "$#!!&$#&." The "word" thus denoted was considered unspeakable in polite society, but now we are expected to use exactly such gibberish-chains as passwords. Little wonder that we might feel like shouting "$#!!&$#&."

As a professional wordsmith, it saddens me that these "words" we're supposed to "pass" when we log onto our email accounts even remotely share the same categorical denomination as the words that actually embody meaning and value: words like "April is the cruelest month" or "The answer is blowin' in the wind." Today's passwords aren't words; I demand a new term for them.

Ancient Roman "watchwords" designed for military security were the antecedents of passwords, Martin Paul Eve writes.[2] We may not want to feel like soldiers confronting an enemy force every time we check our email, but Eve reminds us that the Internet was in fact originally devised by and for the military.

"Password" first surfaced in its current cyberusage ("a sequence of characters, known only to authorized persons, which must be keyed in to gain access to a particular computer, network, file, function, etc."[3]) a half-century ago at a meeting of the American Federation of Information Processing Societies. But passwords long predated the computer age: the first citation as "a selected word or phrase securing admission, recognition, etc., when used by those to whom it is disclosed,"[4] dates to a 1799 translation by Sir Walter Scott: "George shall . . . force the fellow to give him the pass-word."

Francis Plowden's 1811 *The History of Ireland* recounts how "The secret passages to the back of the throne were daily thronged by those, who had the pass word or private key." Thomas Babington Macaulay writes in 1855 of a figure who "longed to be again the president of societies where none could enter without a pass-word." Rolf Boldrewood's 1891 novel *A Colonial Reformer* describes "that fresh, unspoiled, girlish heart to which he alone had the password."[5]

Passwords were once wonderfully colorful: "Open Sesame," from "Ali Baba and the Forty Thieves"; "*Caput draconis*," from Harry Potter; "Swordfish," from the Marx Brothers' *Horse Feathers*. ("Hey, what's a matter, you no understand English? You can't come in here unless you say, 'Swordfish.' Now I'll give you one more guess.")[6] *Get Smart*, the 1960s TV spy comedy, featured such memorable passwords and counterpasswords as "The geese fly high. . . . The frost is on the grass."

That was the golden age of passwords, when those "old-fashioned" phrases illustrated how language could cunningly facilitate access to someplace selective, someplace private and secure. But the ever-growing scale of password piracy suggests that, looking forward, we are doomed to wander haplessly through the babel of $#!!&$#& and 1TiC!AsG. Not only has our privacy been abrogated, but also our expectation that we can use coherent language, words that feel comfortable and familiar, to navigate the world via email.

Email promises instantaneous universal communication, but the army of devious password infiltrators reminds us that our cyberconversations have a dark side: a slough of despond that dampens our innate linguistic enthusiasm by forcing us to pay homage, every time we want to log on, to the toilsome gobbledygook of passwordese. Change them every ninety days; don't repeat used passwords; use a different one for every website; strong, secure passwords should be at least twelve characters long, sixteen is better, including numbers, symbols, and upper- and lower-case letters. The portals to our adventures in language are enveloped in increasingly impenetrable incoherence. (Enveloped! My kingdom for an envelope. Where are the envelopes of yesteryear?)

3 UNREAD

Proceeding through the praxis and telos of email incites kvetching and principled resistance aplenty, but before we go there let us begin with a celebration of the power and the promise of email.

If you have remembered your password and managed to open your inbox, the **lushly thicker type** of the sender's name and subject reveals that some of these messages are not like the others. Most of the emails in most of your folders, already opened and read, has lost this virginal boldness.

"Unread": there is a provocative sublimity in the homograph that you cannot unhear once you have heard it. Instead of "unread" rhyming with "head," think "unread" rhyming with "heed": a verb instead of an adjective. If only I could unread some of the thousands of emails that clog my inbox (not to mention all those interminable Arnold Bennett novels that one of my professors promised, mistakenly, would repay the effort). I could take a trip to Tahiti with all the time I'd reclaim if I could unread things. Like F. Scott Fitzgerald's Benjamin Button (played on-screen by Brad Pitt in an adaptation that is richly worth unseeing), I would shed years of toil and infirmity as I unread my way through an enormity of email.

"Unread" (returning to the adjectival usage) carries a pejorative sneer. An unread person is not knowledgeable, not well-informed: uninstructed, unscholarly, unlettered; an oaf. In *Troilus and Cressida* (the Shakespearean play I would be most inclined to unread), Agamemnon contrasts different character types: "the bold and coward, / The wise and fool, the artist and unread."[1]

The **unread** email, however, is not negative, but affirmative: not stupid, but potentially all-enlightening. **Unread** is why you log on (and on, and on). If you have chosen to take part in this community of communication, this is the best-case scenario—the brass ring, the golden ticket: a new email! There may even be a handful of **unread** emails if you haven't logged on for a few hours. (Which will you read first? Top to bottom? Bottom to top? Will you quickly peruse the as-yet-unmolested missives to decide which looks most exciting, which one you want to read first? Or do you save the best for last?)

"The information comes at night," Martin Amis writes in *The Information.*[2] He's right. When I wake up, the day's largest batch of **unread** email awaits me, and also the best email: from friends and colleagues in Europe, India, Australia (and American insomniacs whose midnight scribblings tend to be more interesting than the norm). Nothing I receive during daylight hours can compete.

More often than not an email is a disappointment: anticlimactic, irrelevant, redundant, or otherwise tedious. It needs some response identical to ones that we have composed a hundred times before and will a thousand times again. An **unread** email is simply a distraction poised to distract, an annoyance waiting to annoy.

Except when it isn't.

Some of them are good. Despite sensibly lowered expectations, we still hope we might receive something, every so often, that is interesting, or funny, or reassuring: that is human, amid (and despite) this mechanical technology of communication that really communicates very little, very imperfectly. "Maybe this time, for the first time . . ." (Liza Minelli in *Cabaret*); "The triumph of hope over experience" (Samuel Johnson). Perhaps this **bold** and fresh new email will be the exception that proves the rule—but what a splendid exception! How many good emails might we dare to hope for? I don't know; when the planets are aligned, maybe 10 percent? Is there anything that could be done to generate more exciting email? What if we sent forth better email ourselves? Are we, perhaps, part of the problem that we blameshift onto every other email writer in the universe? (See Postscript: "How to write a good email.")

The joy of email may reflect serendipity (a long-lost friend who Googled your name and writes to tell you that she thinks everything you have done in the last decade is fascinating!), or anticipation (send off a manuscript that is not execrable and you may hope, every time you check your inbox, for the pleasant sensation of finding a not-impossible acceptance). It may be a business dispute resolved in your favor when a merchant unexpectedly acknowledges fault ("We have credited back to your account the entire sum of $83.20 that you were overcharged for a slice of pizza and a Coke last month in San Francisco; enjoy the free lunch on us!"). It may be a momentous life-course event that probably shouldn't be relegated to email, but increasingly is. ("We're getting married!" "Welcome to the firm." "Get yourself tested.")

"What do people like about email?" I tossed this query out for the reply-all wisdom of the hive.

```
OJ: It's a communication standard not
    controlled by any one large company—so
    anybody, in theory, can run an email
    server themselves (in contrast to, say,
    Facebook, which has all the power).
MGE: Yeah and it's free.
JR: Seconding the benefit of email as
    a standards-based protocol, I also
    appreciate the ability to avoid
    pointless face-to-face encounters and
    (especially) phone conversations with a
    succinct message.
MLD: I love marking important stuff
    "unread"; it keeps it in my mind until I
    do whatever I need to do. I love that it
```

documents conversations with clients — way better than trying to summarize a phone conversation.

GM: I remember the days of traveling long distance to copy documents, photos, etc., for research—with email, I can get a lot more research done in a few days as opposed to weeks or months by post. It's also incredibly faster sending manuscripts back and forth electronically, getting editorial changes quickly, and so on. I don't know how I did without email, but I also don't know how I typed manuscripts on a typewriter!

SF: It isn't the phone. Also, it made faxing nearly obsolete.

DL: I don't have to talk to people. I can communicate on my own schedule. And at work I can document conversations to be referred to later (CYA).

CS: I don't want so many people to be able to call or text me. It's a filter for degrees of communication.

WW: No postage fees.

SL: I love the convenience and malleability of email. An email can be formal or informal, address serious concerns or issue an invitation to a party. We apply for jobs, exchange recipes, and discuss heartache via

email, and it's a medium that withstands
the demands we put on it.

AG: I have a stutter. It's always there
in the background, and usually I don't
notice it. But on the phone it's awful,
debilitating. Not so on email!

SC: I don't have to talk on the phone and
make immediate decisions that may prove
costly. I can think before I respond.

RS: Without it, spam-filled and maddening
as it can be, a whole world of
opportunity would not be available.
Such as working from home, starting
businesses or now more than ever
connecting with and organizing large
groups for civic engagement—think of the
women's march. Email is now kind of old.
Ubiquitous but older, like land lines.
It was the starter dough.

LR: For me, it's all about the virtual
paper trail. It's easy to find exactly
what I communicated and when.

CB: The best thing about email: it's a
naturally searchable database. I rarely
delete emails so if I need to check
on a schedule arrangement or remember
something I said, or prove that I didn't
promise something to someone, I have a
record of everything.

If it may seem that I have come to bury email rather than to praise it, still I begin with the glass half full, the "weird love-hate dynamic everyone seems to have with e-mail," as John Pavlus describes it: "We've let it seep into every nook and cranny of our lives, and we resent its presence. But we also crave it."[3]

Larry Rosen describes our evolving psychological relationship with technology: "E-mail has become an approach-avoid conflict for us. We know there might be a gem in [our inbox] somewhere right now, but we have to sift through all the crap to find it. . . . The accessibility of email and its unpredictable pleasures stimulate our brain's 'seeking' circuits, which are mediated by the neurotransmitter dopamine, which helps the brain assign incentive salience to stimuli that might provide a reward."[4] "We may despise our inboxes (and 99% of what's in them)," Pavlus explains, "but we're neurochemically compelled to make sure that there isn't something potentially important or pleasurable lurking in there this time. And then five minutes from now. And then again. And again."[5]

The triumph of hope over experience.

"Email is still the best thing on the Internet," writes Alexis Madrigal. "You can't kill email! It's the cockroach of the Internet, and I mean that as a compliment. This resilience is a good thing." He calls email "a tremendous, decentralized, open platform on which new, innovative things can and have been built. . . . Email is a refugee from the open, interoperable, less-controlled 'web we lost.' It's an exciting landscape of freedom amidst the walled gardens of social networking and messaging services."[6]

Email is writing, and I'm an English professor, so I love writing, and ergo I love email. (:-/ People are sending more email than ever, so people are doing more writing than ever—that's great. Writing helps people think in a better way (than not-writing): more composed, organized, sophisticated. Sure, some people write some lousy emails, but if everyone were already a great writer I'd be out of a job.

Also: email is magic. It flies through the air. It somehow (I think) goes up into the actual heavens and bounces off of a satellite (perhaps?) and then shoots back down to earth. Think of our words, banal and profound, sacred and profane, rebounding across the cosmos. Maybe we will all be better off for dousing the cosmos in this expansive network of ideas and connections. Or maybe we are just making ourselves all the more vulnerable to hackers, spies, and totalitarian regimes. Maybe this insanely profuse exchange of information via email is inherently dangerous, as we of the Anthropocene have shown ourselves to be in so many other ways. If we weren't spending so much time emailing everyone everything everywhere, would we be more connected to our own immediate local (real!) ecospaces instead of our infinite imaginary cyberspaces? Would we figure out how to live in our moments, more sensibly, more sustainably? Maybe we would read *Sand County Almanac* and *Silent Spring* instead of tracking our

Amazon shipments hourly and overloading our Outlook calendars that "create events" (what hath God wrought?!) out of email. Maybe we would stir our compost heaps, or harvest rainwater, or walk somewhere instead of obsessively checking our inboxes.

But maybe not.

Everything happens for a reason. There's a special providence in the fall of a sparrow. Perhaps our task is simply to figure out what email is for: the readiness is all; the **unread**iness is all.

Think of the **unread** email as one that does not (at least not *yet,* not until it is opened and read) embody all the faults of extant email. It could be everything that no other email has yet been. If "spamming" means wasting other people's time online, Finn Brunton writes,

> can we imagine a contrary verb? That is, can we build media platforms that respect our attention and the finite span of our lives expended at the screen? How would all the things transacted on a computer screen look if they took our time—this existential resource of waking, living hours in a fragile body—as seriously as they could? A careful arrangement of meaningful information relative to our unique interests, needs, and context.[7]

Spam, email's worst-case scenario, tantalizes Brunton with its ideal, if unlikely, antithesis: something (careful, graceful, interesting) that merits our consideration and that thrills us to transform from **unread** to read.

But how to compose such an email?

4 COMPOSE (DRAFT)

Really? "Compose" an email? As Antonín Dvořák composed the *New World Symphony*? As Georgia O'Keeffe composed her erotobotanical canvases? Is our terminology perhaps a bit presumptuous here? Why not just "write"?—and even that might be too self-congratulatory, overstating the accomplishment. "Spew" or "disgorge" might be more fitting. "Eruct."

Composing, according to the *OED*, seems much grander than what I do all day to generate email:

To make by putting together parts or elements: to make up, form, frame, fashion, construct, produce. To constitute; to be the constituents or material of. To construct (in words); to produce in literary form, to write as author. *Music.* To invent and put into proper form. *Print.* To put together (types) so as to form words and blocks of words; to set up (type); to set up (an article, a page) in type. To put together (parts or elements) so as to make up a whole; *spec.* in artistic use, To arrange artistically the elements of a landscape or painting. To construct artistically. To arrange (any matter) properly or successfully; to settle.

However unpromisingly, let us compose ourselves and then compose our email as best we can, trying to ignore the gargantuan anxiety of compositional influence hovering over our shoulders.

Ready, steady, go. Pen to paper. No, that's not right; no one has ever composed a handwritten draft of an email.

Begin the beguine. Fingers to keyboard. Typos are OK—autocorrect will catch them . . . or not. Start with the subject. Don't enter the recipient's address yet, in case you accidentally hit the wrong button and fire off a premature ejaculation, an *epistle interruptus*; we have all done it. ("Button"? There are no buttons to be found here. Why, in these cybertimes, are our figurations so laughably archaic?)

Take your time. Don't compose immediately or she'll think you wrote back too quickly: you couldn't have had time to read her whole email. And if you respond to a 2:12 email at 2:14, she'll think you don't have anything else to do on a Tuesday afternoon but stalk your inbox and respond like a trained seal. Cool your heels.

But if I respond, then this will be done with—one less thing to worry about.

Unless she writes back, responding to my response, a dialogue that may expand ad infinitum.

But I can compose an email that brooks no response.

Maybe later. Abort. Quit. Discard. Yes, OK, fine, Save as Draft. Resume anon, when I am more composed.

5 SUBJECT

The subject line asks the composer to describe: what is the email about? More broadly, I ask here: *what is email about?* Taking a detour from sniffing out the attributes of email as an object, consider here how it functions as a subject, when cultural creators write email stories or sing email songs, when they theorize email. Do artists, writers, and musicians generate anything that helps us *place* email, understand it, appraise it in terms of the kinds of values and tropes (e.g., beauty, repulsion, good-and-evil, imagination, desire, anagnorisis, catharsis, power and disempowerment, subversion) that we habitually use to read an artifact through culture?

Let me begin by diminishing expectations: email's aesthetic footprint is scant. At first glance, email-as-art seems unspectacular; attempting to put the best possible face on it, I may be able to bump this up to "quizzical." *Deus ex machina* is the classical term for when something like email contributes an unexpected plot significance: god from the machine. There are, certainly, lots of machines around, infinitely more than when ancient storytellers came up with the idea, "let's have a machine save the day." But are they remotely godlike, these email "machines" in contemporary stories, music, and art?

The subject of email, the plots and aesthetics of email, seem constrained by the actual fodder of email, which Stanley Solomon characterizes as "bland, minimalistic, occasionally incoherent, and almost always singleminded."[1] It is inherently

> informational, never intentionally esthetic in design and, as far as my experience goes, never esthetic even by accident—as if a graceful, insightful, or intricate sentence were blocked by a style checker programmed to delete anything that is not ordinary, redundant, excessive, or illiterate.[2]

One might hypothesize that a medium as widespread as email should have a more significant cultural corpus than it does. Almost four billion users[3] send 2.7 million emails every second.[4] Mustn't at least a few of them follow in the pawsteps of those proverbial monkeys from the statistical parable who will eventually type *King Lear*?[5] And yet we have no *E-lectra*, *E-neid*, or *E-dipus;* no *E.-T.* or *E-vita*, no *E.- of Eden*, no email exploits or eminences.

Still, we can find art in email, email in art: at least some practitioners, calling themselves "email artists," would have us believe so. Email art grows out of an earlier "mail art" phenomenon, disseminated through the postal service: an egalitarian and conceptual resistance against the institutional elitism of galleries and museums featuring doctored postcards, envelopes embellished with doodles, artisanal ink-stamp designs, and found-art distributed freely and randomly.

Mail art projects were often described as "networked," so it makes sense that the movement evolved to include email art.[6] In an arcane corner of the art world, a 1997 'zine titled "RE: THE E-MAIL-ART & INTERNET-ART MANIFESTO," Belgian mail artist Guy Bleus invited two dozen collaborators to email him statements on how art could intersect with email. They responded:

> I don't take part in e-mail art projects. E-mail is a tool for research and communication. I subscribe to several research lists with over 200 or so items a day as well as another 30 or 40 personal messages. When I travel, sorting the mail takes an average of two hours for every day away. Like telefax, email should be a tool and not an intrusion. I value messages from people who communicate directly with me as an individual. I don't want email communications from people who see me as part of a network and I don't want email from artists who are only communicating with me merely because I have email. Privacy is an important human right. I value my privacy and I don't use email for network art projects. – Ken Friedman

//x. Now we can attach a picture, a sound or a video to our e-mail: a can of beer would be better!// – Charles Francois

Expose the whole fucking edifice. Everything comes back as merchandise. Subvert the dominant position, let's all be on top! –Steven Perkins

electronic exchange is like the model of an atomic system—spirals, smashings, swirling, and linear acceleration. Electronic communications sometimes cause a rash of energy, other times they dissipate into space and nothingness. – Daniel Plunkett

According to my thinking, e-mail is not an umbrella for mail artists. It is only an emergency form of address, one that is utilitarian and quick. Snail mail is the only mail for mail artists. – Judith A. Hoffberg

Signs travel here as connection directs the weight of freedom as a dream disappears but won't give up. – Spencer Selby

It ain't MAIL ART, if it isn't mailed. E-mail is networking, NOT mail-art. – Anna Banana

> e-mail-art swarms and buzzes total
> contact fades the self becoming
> eyestrain headache, falls away... –John
> M. Bennett
>
> E Mail Art is instantaneous, inexpensive
> and broad based, but lacks the rustle and
> texture of human communication. –Joel S.
> Cohen[7]

Asked to consider the Venn-overlap between email and art, these artists offer varied and contradictory insights, from the ridiculous to the sublime. François: Attach beer. Banana: No art here. Hoffberg: ditto. Friedman: I prefer not to. Perkins: Blow it the fuck up! Bennett: email gives you a headache. In a camp of resistance, many artists clung to analogue conventionality.

But a few techno-optimists are open to plunging into the avant-garde. Plunkett imagines the subject's inherent scientific underpinnings as a possibly animating force, celebrating a random kinetic energy that email art may, potentially, manifest—"spirals, smashings, swirling, and linear acceleration"—while acknowledging too the possibility of failure, as the enterprise may "dissipate into space and nothingness."

Cohen and Selby occupy a middle ground, agnostics, but still interested to see how the experiment unfolds. Cohen conceives email art as "instantaneous, inexpensive and broad based"—all seminal values of mail art—but notes also that it "lacks the rustle and texture of human communication": a keenly phrased assessment of what may have been lost not just as mail art became email art but, more broadly, as mail became email.

When Selby writes, "Signs travel here as connection directs the weight of freedom as a dream disappears but won't give up," we may detect imaginative empowerment lurking in this abstract dictum. "Signs travel": that's good. Signs are resonant, and traveling signs would bring the images, the lessons, to a wider audience. You don't have to travel to them (in the MoMA or the Pompidou): they deliver right to your doorstep . . . er, inbox. "Connection," I think, denotes email, and "connection directs the weight of freedom" implies that a sender, an artist, can "direct"—can create, and can gain agency by tapping into this connection. Freedom (= art, knowledge, power, self-determination) is weighty, and the "attachments" in this model of email transmission may be large and unwieldy ones; they may compete with junk email and hypercirculated meaninglessness. Email is freedom, but also, it is weighted down with the blather of the universe. Selby describes how "a dream disappears but won't give up," a tight phrase that captures the ambivalence of the early email era in which anyone may send (almost) anything to (almost) anyone (almost) freely and (almost) immediately, a phenomenon that once seemed like a dream, and now may seem more like a dreary fugue, but he is right that email "won't give up." It's here for the long haul.

I can read your most intimate emails

and potentially pass them on

A simple search would allow strangers to find everything about
you, your friends

and family

FIGURE 8 Email art. Elsa Philippe, *I am you all* [*sic*] (detail), 2018.
With permission of the artist.

Elsa Philippe, a contemporary email artist, says her "ideas
are coming from everyday life" as she explores "how new
technologies affect human behaviour and daily life rituals"
in the "chaotic and grotesque world" of a "society addicted
to new technologies."[8] Her 2018 work *I am you all* [*sic*] uses
the format and tenor of email, its tropes and threats, to
create a word-portrait that aestheticizes the global/universal
sensibilities of email. "I am colonizing one of your chief
platforms of interaction with the world," she announces
self-consciously in her ominous pronouncement about the
zeitgeist of email: "You will feel the need to understand me";
"I will gain all control"; "depression / heightened anxiety /
loss of confidence / sleeplessness"; "your email account is
the nexus of the modern world / and I am going to steal it."
"HOSTAGE / you will email to your own email account,"[9] she
writes . . . which, as I have already admitted, I often do.

There is a Museum of Email; it's online at http://email-museum.com/. "Computer-based communications technologies have revolutionized human experience," its homepage effuses:

> The impact has been remarkable, and breathtaking. Email initiated the revolution. . . . The roller-coaster innovations continue, exciting and unpredictable. Most of the early innovators are still alive, and the electronic record of the technologies' evolution is rich. We thus have a wonderful opportunity to record the development of digital communications for posterity. . . . We can record the revolution in a way that wasn't possible with earlier innovations in human communications that shook the world, such as the book, the postal system, and the telephone. Hence *The Museum of Email & Digital Communications*.[10]

(I take umbrage at the implied critique of postal museums. I have visited a dozen: all brilliantly exhibiting their revolution, they leave this one in the dust.) The new phenomenon of "virtual museums," infusing cyberspace with cultural education, may provide archival and documentary platforms for critical reflection and analysis. A few of them work well, but here, curators seem to have lost interest in the project about five years ago: they've left up a hodgepodge of blogs, blurbs, and reports on things like the development of corporate email and the origin of emoticons. ((→.←)) As often when email aspires beyond its reach and tries to achieve a grander status for itself, the result is disappointing: the website's platitudes provide a weak foundation forestalling any more sophisticated museological attention. The crowds clearly don't flock here, probably because they know that it's basically still just email: notes, annoyances, trivialities, spam. There are a lot of dead links here in the Museum of Email. So it goes.

Incisive and engaging literary considerations of email are rare. Maybe it's just too soon, and we'll have to wait another generation or two before more writers begin to set their sights, energetically and thoughtfully, on the meaning of email: peeking behind the curtain and digging into its guts to produce a resonant aesthetic, or textual, or ethical, or semiotic exploration of the medium.

Two anomalies are Adaobi Tricia Nwaubani's novel *I Do Not Come to You by Chance* (2009) and Elif Batuman's *The Idiot* (2017). Set in the 1990s, Batuman portrays a college relationship in the early days of email where the awkwardness of this new technology mirrors the awkwardness of Selin's courtship with Ivan (who is not primo boyfriend material, but, to his credit, writes a pretty mean email). The novel opens with Selin's recollection:

> I didn't know what email was until I got to college. I had heard of email, and knew that in some sense I would "have" it. "You'll be so fancy," said my mother's sister, who had married a computer scientist, "sending your e, mails." She emphasized the "e" and paused before "mail."[11]

Batuman describes Selin's dawning awareness of what email was and how it was coming to inhabit her world:

> Insofar as I had any idea about it at all, I had imagined that email would resemble faxing, and would involve a printer. But there was no printer. There was another world. You could access it from certain computers, which were scattered throughout the ordinary landscape, and looked no different from regular computers. Always there, unchanged, in a configuration nobody else could see, was a glowing list of messages from all the people you knew, and from people you didn't know, all in the same letters, like the universal handwriting of thought, or of the world.[12]

Selin is drawn to Ivan as their email correspondence blossoms, although on some level she is captivated more by the email than the emailer. "Part of what Selin likes so much about Ivan is that he writes these pretentious things, about clowns and hell and insanity, without even caring that they're pretentious," Batuman explains in an interview. "Email enabled a whole new kind of pretentiousness." Ivan's long emails are "really specific and cryptic at the same time, and it's like, all those things were waiting there in him and all she had to do was write to him and he would tell her. That's something I remember being really exciting when email was new. It felt like email made manifest this whole side of everyone that you just never saw before, because there was no email to manifest it."[13]

Nwaubani's novel depicts "419ers," Nigerians who get rich through email scams (section 419 of the country's criminal code deals with fraud), targeting a prospective Western chump, a "mugu" in the local pidgin. Her title, a phrase that might introduce one of these bogus emails, is inaccurate: in fact, the scammers choose their email recipients absolutely at random, by the hundreds and thousands, the great majority of whom will delete the email immediately while a small (but highly profitable) number send money hoping for a stake in the millions of dollars that a deposed or deceased politician left sitting inaccessible in a Swiss bank account, recoverable only with the help of an American collaborator, who will reap an easy 10 or 20 percent of the profits, and for now, just needs to send a $7500 wire payment for filing and processing the requisite forms and fees.

```
I DO NOT COME TO YOU BY CHANCE. UPON MY
QUEST FOR A TRUSTED AND RELIABLE FOREIGN
BUSINESS MAN OR COMPANY, I WAS GIVEN
YOUR CONTACT BY THE NIGERIAN CHAMBER OF
COMMERCE AND INDUSTRY. I HOPE THAT YOU CAN
BE TRUSTED TO HANDLE A TRANSACTION OF THIS
MAGNITUDE. FOLLOWING THE SUDDEN DEATH OF
MY HUSBAND . . .[14]
```

Her morality tale develops an elaborate and somewhat convincing situational ethics to justify these scams: foreign opportunists have taken so much wealth from Africa for so long that this fraud is merely a small payback; greedy and gullible, the mugus are hoist with their own petards, and the amounts they lose are trivial compared to the scope of the country's profound poverty. The ploys exploit the mugus' preconceptions of pervasive African corruption, so the 419ers see poetic justice: consdescending Westerners get what they deserve from the Nigerians they disrespect. And as much as Nigerians resent Westerners' haughty presumptions about bureaucratic corruption and economic desperation, Nwaubani's story shows that, unfortunately, those beliefs are actually accurate; so a smart and hardworking character like her protagonist Kingsley, a trained chemical engineer, resorts to fraud because there are few legitimate professional opportunities. And while some of the con artists' loot buys Rolexes and Lexuses, some also goes for building schools, maintaining orphanages, and supporting large families and communities.

As an American who receives such emails by the dozens and deletes them without spending more than a second wondering why they exist and how stupid someone would have to be to get suckered into this fraud, I find Nwaubani's story an insightful counterpoint, exploring the other side of this common scam-spam. She shows that the subject here is not so much email as it is imperialism and global inequity. And while the fraudulent emails are a confidence game, they are also a genre, a voice of resistance, even an art form, resonating with a potent and (to me) unexpectedly nuanced subtext about connections between Africa and the West in the networks of global cyberspace.

Profusely if unmomentously, email infuses movies and songs—it's front and center in *You've Got Mail*, Nora Ephron's charming 1998 romcom starring Meg Ryan and Tom Hanks, and "E-mail My Heart," from Britney Spears's 1999 debut album . . . *Baby One More Time*. To begin at the bottom: Spears's hit song shines a light on email in no meaningful way whatsoever as she revisits the well-trod angst of romantic bickering. It has been so long (hours!) since her boyfriend went away, she sings, and she keeps checking her social media to see how he is doing. He doesn't answer the phone— she guesses he wants to be left alone. The fight seems to have been her fault, but, she is sorry (oh so sorry!). Contrite, she pleads for one more chance: "E-mail my heart / And say our love will never die."[15]

Here is the singer's own revelation of what moved her to croon about email: "'E-mail My Heart' is, like, a song everyone can relate to, you know . . . everyone has been doing e-mails. And it's 'E-mail My Heart,' so everyone can relate to it."[16] "What's weird is that email and online culture weren't even *that* nascent in 1999," as Jordan Bassett notes in his analysis of this song; "they had already, surely, entered the lives of most people in a fairly everyday manner—and yet the lyrics still make a bodge of the terminology. I can see you in my mind, Britney sings, '*coming on the line*.' Coming on the line? Who says that?"[17]

Reviewer Kristie Rohwedder writes: "The lyrics were dated literally seconds after Britney recorded the song, naysayers nay say. And as if the corny lyrics weren't bad enough, the song is forgettable," she pronounces, adding sarcastically: "The phrase 'E-mail my heart' is a sentiment that truly captures the essence of humankind."[18] Music writer Maitri Mehta's exegesis begins: "Wait . . . what? At first it's like, OK, Britney just wants her boyfriend to email her back. But then you wonder: Is it a metaphor? Does she want him to email her heart back to her, because he currently has it, or is the recipient of the email Britney's heart? This song is still a head-scratcher almost 20 years later."[19] (Possibly of relevance: in 2006 Spears split from her husband, Kevin Federline, by text message.)

There's a sizeable corpus of musical email, generally manifesting a Spearsian caliber of lyricism:

"E-mail" (Pet Shop Boys, 2002): Send me an e-mail / that says "I love you."

"When You Get to Asheville" (Steve Martin and Edie Brickell, 2013): Send me an email, / Tell me how you're doing.

"Bug A Boo" (Destiny's Child, 1999): Have AOL make my email stop / Cause you a bug a boo.

"Missed Calls" (Mac Miller, 2011): Baby I got missed calls and e-mails, / All going into details about how you just not happy.

"Feels Like Summer" (Weezer, 2017): I'm a Libra, if it matters / Shattered by an email.

"Gettin' Up" (Q-Tip, 2008): Sent you a message, sent you an email / Hasty decisions we made still prevail.

"Fanmail" (TLC, 1999): Said I got an e-mail today / Kinda thought that you forgot about me.

"Send Me an Email" (Tila Tequilla, T-Pain, J-Shin, 2006): Sent me an email / with all the details.[20]

My favorite least-favorite is Alice Cooper's 2003 "Bye Bye, Baby" where the Methuselah of heavy metal sings: "Bye bye baby, please check your email." You get the drift. The musical emails are contrived. They may vaguely and inelegantly broach the need to communicate as an element of the need to live and love—we need to connect with other people to be happy. There's a noteworthy leitmotif of malaise in these songs: a relationship hanging on an email is probably living on borrowed time. Mostly, email as a trope is blandly robotic. Email is a system, a tool; it's not an art, nor a muse. "E-mail messages flirt with their own insignificance," Philip Stevick writes; "It is the nature of the form that they should do so."[21] Object lesson: don't sing about email.

"You've got mail": the mellifluous voice belonged to Elwood Edwards, whose fifteen minutes of fame started ticking when his wife, who worked for the company that became AOL, volunteered him for the job of announcing each incoming message's arrival. In the UK, a variant jingle featured a sultry Joanna Lumley, who said, more formally: "You have email."

Elwood's eloquent elocution eventually got annoying, so now messages are heralded with a subtler ping (or ring or bing). Today Elwood drives an Uber but will still, upon request, happily intone his famous phrase.[22] Nostalgic aficionados can easily find (Google) and install an mp3 file of Edwards's original pronouncement.

Ephron's film (which credits Edwards) stars Ryan and Hanks as Joe and Kathleen, two delightful souls destined to be sweethearts who are, alas, on the surface, incompatible: she's a small-time bookseller, and he's a mogul whose expanding megachain threatens to bankrupt her charming boutique. In a twist of irony worthy of O. Henry, they hate each other in person but when they accidentally and anonymously hook up on email, they reveal their true selves and fall in love.

They exchange incredibly rich, honest emails with (as each believes the other to be) a stranger, about their deepest emotional anxieties and desires, because they are lonely in real life. "The odd thing about this form of communication," Kathleen writes to Joe, "is that you're more likely to talk about nothing than something but I just want to say that all this nothing has meant more to me than so many somethings. So thanks."[23]

The world of email is idealistically depicted as a place where people can make vital, authentic connections. Our actual social existence is plagued with hubris, posturing, pride and prejudice, Ephron's story suggests, but email strips that all away and lets us be our simple, essential selves. Could this possibly be true? I don't think you'd see such a conceit today: it was a utopian fantasy of the early email era (eee). Another romance from this period, McKenzie Wark and Kathy Acker's *I'm Very into You* (published in 2015, but containing their correspondence from 1995 to 1996), presents a similarly naïve optimism about the transcendent authenticity and imaginative fecundity of email relationships. Acker's executor Matias Viegener edited this book long after her death, noting in his introduction that "There's an intensity here forged in part by the medium itself, the then new medium of email. Today's reader will notice the writer's occasional references to a technology which has entirely naturalized itself for us."[24] This naturalization, Viegener implies, dampens the avant-garde novelty—the excitement of a blank slate, which dissipated rather quickly as we became blasé about email—that resonates also in Ephron's movie and Batuman's retrospective memories from the eee.

Finally, there is a large and predictable genre of email-as-subject anachronistically, or retroactively. "If only they had email in 1810," one webpage laments; "They do now"—and it goes on to reconstruct what Anne Elliot's and Mr. Darcy's inboxes would look like.[25] *McSweeney's* imagines Shakespeare's email, where all the world's a stage, and all the men and women merely players:

```
they have their exits and their entrances;
so let's reconnect on this over the weekend.
```

And

> Shall I compare thee to a summer's day?
> Feel free to reach out if you have further
> Q's.[26]

You get the point. Such parodies depict a forced merger of real language—good words, well-thought-out writing—with email language, which is presumed, by contrast, to be vacant. "Shakespeare's email" is where worlds meet, and while our contemporary vernacular gets the last word, it is not the best word. The (quickly tiresome) comic device demonstrates people's need to assert some kind of relation, however cringeworthy, between how people used to write in some golden age of literature and how we do now in a world tainted by pervasive cybercommunication. Even as such spoofs unsparingly mock the vacuous nowness of email, still, they assert the importance of sustaining a connection to predigital traditions, and of somehow carving out a space in email that can accommodate some remnant of those traditions.

6 ATTACHMENT

Just as we once put a photograph, an invoice, or a resumé in an envelope with a cover letter, now we attach it to an email. A prEmail missive was an object that collated and carried smaller individual objects. But those objects are no longer *enclosed*, inside: they're *attached*, alongside. The paper clip icon indicates how the user is encouraged to think about the attachment's objectness. (Paper clips have long been recognized as an ineffective technology of attachment, superseded by binder clips and butterfly wire-clamps; I wonder why email iconographers haven't gotten the memo on this.)

An attachment may be too large: files over 25 MB could bounce back, though clouds, Dropbox, and file compression are workarounds. Some wary recipients may block attachments, which could be dangerous: like a Trojan horse, they can hide viruses, worms, malware (there is actually a type of malware called "Trojan") that sneaks through your computer's gates when your guard is down and ransacks the entire city.

But an attachment is a pretty easy way to send digitized objects: texts and images, contracts, forms, theater tickets, newsletters, letters of recommendation. The manuscript of this book will soon be sent as an email attachment to my editors, with a subject line stating, simply, "Email," and a pithy message, "See attached." Many trips to my office have been rendered unnecessary because a colleague was able to scan-and-attach something which I "docusigned" and attached back to her. Especially if we don't print them out, attachments help reduce our carbon footprints.

Students send me their final essays as email attachments at noon on the day they are due, so I no longer pace impatiently in my office waiting for that last laggard student to dawdle in. The assignment will come when it comes: ping.

Maybe we are not as attached to attachments as we might think. I would say that at least one-quarter of emails I receive referencing attachments do not in fact have them. (Absent-minded professors!) Sometimes a second email arrives swiftly with the subject line, always: "Sorry, forgot the attachment." But sometimes it's up to me to actively request the missing file. "Don't see attachment here?" I write, helping the distracted sender to save face (maybe it's my confusion), more polite than what I would like to say, which is, "You forgot the attachment." Perhaps it fell off on its way from your outbox to my inbox; possibly that metaphorical paper clip has been metaphorically overused and has lost its metaphorical grip.

Did anyone ever receive an empty envelope followed by another with a letter saying, "Sorry, I forgot the letter?"

I attach my lecture notes in an email I send myself every day before I leave home, so that if I misplace my hard copy

I can read them on my phone. Increasingly, we use our phones for engaging email. It's not ideal—the screens and keypads are too small ("keypads"? there are no keys here, and no pad), and my middle-aged thumbs are less adroit than they might be, but it serves in a pinch. Email, now, is always with us: in our pockets, at our bedsides, whether we are at home or at work or out dancing or in Iceland. I can still say "Temporarily away from my email," but it has become figurative, aspirational: we may pretend to be "away" from email, but email is not away from us. We are attached. We are the attachment.

7 SEND

"That letter will be appreciated," promises a Depression-era WPA poster commemorating National Letter Writing Week. A stylized mailman, strong and sleek, holds a letter in one hand and rings the recipient's doorbell with the other. Staring intently at the letter, he makes sure the address matches his location. Across his torso, like the breastplate on a coat of armor, his carrier pouch holds many more letters—a mail of letters!—which will certainly be appreciated by people up and down the street. Do we detect the slight crack of a playful grin on his face, signifying his joy that, despite the tough times, he has a good steady and meaningful job? Or is that line just a shadow from one of the letters in his pouch? It's ambiguous, but either way the image conveys the contentment of the middleman in the delivery system, and equally, the simple pleasure of the delivered object itself.

The mail carrier is the neighborhood's linchpin and the mail he carries, letter by letter, day after day, is its lifeblood. (Remember Virginia Woolf: "When the post knocks and the letter comes always the miracle seems repeated." W. H.

FIGURE 9 Federal Arts Project poster, c. 1940. Library of Congress Prints and Photographs Division, WPA Poster Collection.

Auden, too, loved getting mail: "none will hear the postman's knock / Without a quickening of the heart, / For who can bear to feel himself forgotten?"[1]) As an object, this letter is small and distinct, exciting, reliable. The poster conveys mail-as-object and also mail-as-infrastructure: both a singular letter and, representing the larger system, a group of letters. The envelopes are different sizes, but not very different. The stamps, signifying the economy of the mail, are rendered as identical brown patches (the same color as the mailman's ear and nose, and also the doorbell, emphasizing the system's well-tuned interfaces).

The mailman's outfit is traditional postal livery, a spritely baby blue trimmed with a darker azure accent. His arms and legs are human but also, almost, mechanical. (Still today, postal carriers always have muscular physiques from all the walking they do.) The semiotic aura is trustworthy, patriotic, community-minded. Not just that letter "will be appreciated," but so much more as well: social bonds, challenged during the Depression, may be sustained and strengthened by the letter, the cheap postage, the happy mail carrier, and the industrial fleet that conveys these letters back and forth across the country and beyond. Mail service meant prosperity, social progress, integrity. It meant connection: as Auden noted, we are not forgotten.

But now, mail is outdone by email. One phrase—a sleazy, obnoxious cheap shot—singlehandedly punctures the postal service's storied legacy:

Snail mail.

This term, this anti-brand, cuts to the heart of what mail had been. At the risk of belaboring the obvious: "The phrase refers to the lag-time between dispatch of a letter and its receipt, versus the virtually instantaneous dispatch and delivery of its electronic equivalent, email."[2] *Urban Dictionary* kicks the corpse: "Snail Mail: Tax funded delivery of trash to your apartment daily, except on Sundays and certain holidays, all year long." Usage example: "My recycle bin is full of snail mail."[3]

The object that the WPA image conveyed with such reassuring certainty is more complex and attenuated today. Mail used to be consummately human: humans writing to other humans, facilitated by humans. This colossal enterprise was celebrated in the famous (though unofficial) creed: "Neither snow nor rain nor heat nor gloom of night stays these couriers from the swift completion of their appointed rounds." The words, borrowed from Herodotus's *Histories*, originally described the ancient Persian Empire's courier service known as the Angarium.

And today: how do we express the pride, the labor, the power of our communications? The endurance of the operation? The historical roots of the tradition? "That letter will be appreciated," the mailman promised. Will that email be appreciated?

Can email fit into our neighborhoods and our culture as the mail-pouched neither-snow-nor-rain corps did? How do we compensate for the absence of the person in the blue uniform? How are email messages related to our social organization? Could we imagine a commemoration of National Email Writing Week? What image, what ethos, could possibly illustrate for email, as the WPA poster does for mail, the system, the process, the value, the currency, the circulation, the cultural ubiquity, of this object?

Mail was run by the government as a public service, a cornerstone of our civic infrastructure. Email is run by . . . Google? Microsoft? ISPs? The FCC? Our employers? Our universities? Our cell phones? Possibly our cable television providers? Netflix? I can never remember who is in charge of what in my technological life: it wouldn't shock me to learn that I am getting double-billed for some of this—or for all of it.

One of those nebulous tech conglomerates, Honeywell, created a magazine advertisement forty years after the WPA poster, featuring a chump who is as unsettled in his job as the earlier citizen-mailman is stable in his. The 1940 tagline—a direct, assured statement of fact: "That letter will be appreciated"—has become, in 1980, a question, and an oddly unsettling one, possibly unanswerable: "What the heck is electronic mail?"

The mailman's steady composure as he walks his route from house to house through the community contrasts surreally with the disaffected, discombobulated, deranged sensibility of the suit-and-tie-guy who is intellectually and existentially overwhelmed (I don't think that's too strong a reading of this tableau) by the brave new world that has invaded his office space. This advertisement is contemporaneous with

FIGURE 10 What the heck? Advertisement, c. 1980, used with Honeywell's permission.

the invention of the Taser, which may help explain what's happening to him.

He is absolutely freaked out. His snazzy tie, shag carpet, and knock-off Scandinavian moderne office desk cannot sufficiently prepare him to engage the new technology that is going to rock his world. The force of "electronics," as depicted in this ad, is terrifyingly uncontrollable. If the man in the blue livery who brought the letters (swiftly completing his appointed rounds) represented human-scaled dependability and connection, this newfangled electrowhatsit seems to embody everything that is alien and incoherent.

Honeywell's "Electronic Mail" is not yet what we now know as email—they were still working on their clunky Level 6 operating system, which used "Multics" (Multiplexed Information and Computing Service), a rudimentary early OS that had an "Executive Mail" interface. The ad explains:

Electronic Mail is a term that's been bandied about data processing circles for years.

Simply put, it means high-speed information transportation.

One of the most advanced methods is terminals talking to one another.

Your mailbox is the terminal on your desk. Punch a key and today's correspondence and messages are displayed instantly.

Need to notify people immediately of a fast-breaking development? Have your messages delivered to their terminal mailboxes electronically, across the hall or around the world.

Electronic Mail is document distribution that's more timely, accurate, and flexible than traditional methods.

The flash tracks of this terrifying electrostatic discharge have brought imminent physical terror into the office of this poor balding mid-level executive; will it give him a heart attack? Are we actually watching him go into cardiac arrest in the frozen moment of this ad? Why would Honeywell want to depict his trauma in their prophecy of the coming technology? Maybe his replacement will be less unsettled by electronic mail: Honeywell's subliminal suggestion for corporate America is to electrocute the old farts and make way for staff who won't ask stupid questions like "What the heck is electronic mail?" Send him packing.[4] Send forth lightning and scatter the enemy.[5] Send all my plagues upon thine heart.[6] Send in the clowns.[7]

Semiotically, the agon between mail and email plays out by counterpoising the depictions of the actual letter, *l'objet proper*, in 1940 vs. 1980. The WPA object is simple, solid, easily recognizable, and of a piece (geometrically, chromatically, compositionally) with the rest of the process, the organizational phenomenon of postal delivery, in which it is the central element. Forty years later, the object is not being delivered by any human hand, nor is the hand in this ad even willing or able to touch it. The object formerly known as "mail" has become fuzzy, blurry, scary, luminescent, ghostly, deathly, in the incomprehensible power and terror it seems to wield. Avoid. Recoil. Cloaked in an ominous (radioactive?) glow, it hovers over the desk: you can't see who it's from or what it says as it zings electrically across the office like a supercharged nanorocket gone berserk.

When people sent letters, everyone knew exactly where each object of mail went and how it got there. "We have no idea about where email goes when we hit send," writes Simon Garfield. "We couldn't track the journey if we cared to; in the end, it's just another vanishing."[8]

8 INBOX

To examine our inboxes is to examine our lives: our desires and dreams, our families and careers, our status, our networks and our social groupings, our projects, our commerce, our politics, our secrets/lies/fetishes. Inboxes are anthropological goldmines, textual archives, psychological case studies, waiting to be plumbed and probed for the expansive cultural, ethical, epistemological, and ontological insights lurking therein. On second thought: they are probably not *waiting to be probed*, but *actually being probed*, scanned and algorithmatized, by Google, Amazon, the National Security Agency, the Russians, Julian Assange, employers, ex-lovers who remember your password, current lovers who install surveillance software on your laptop to monitor emails to your ex-lover/next lover, hackers who create fake networks on any public wifi you log onto, and/or anyone else who cares to discover whatever "secrets" you are secreting into the tubes. It makes more sense to assume your email is a public document than to cling to improbable expectations of privacy. The Post Office made a point of delivering our letters sealed, intact. But the email overseers can read through our inboxes at will without us being any the wiser, and they let others look too: just to skim through until they find the word (the *object*) "bicycle" or "chainsaw," and then try to sell us this object . . . for our own good, because they think we might want one. How convenient!

Consider how much of your energy, not to mention your eyesight, is being sucked away, byte by byte, by a deadening deluge of ill-composed blather, corporate groupthink, commercial come-ons, and other meaningless Internet flotsam. Are inboxes becoming bionic appendages of our own consciousness? "Dispatches from the minds of others . . . shot right into the working nerve centers of our new surrogate brains" is how one frazzled correspondent describes the ceaseless barrage. "It's not just the number of messages but the feeling that somebody has *invaded your head*."[1]

Is it too cynical to substitute "email" for "Communist" in Base Commander Jack D. Ripper's screed from *Dr. Strangelove*? "I can no longer sit back and allow Communist infiltration, Communist indoctrination, Communist subversion, and the international Communist conspiracy to sap and impurify all of our precious bodily fluids."[2]

Your work life and your social life, your grown-up self and your college self, your single salad days and your soccer-dad phase, all weirdly conjoined in your inbox, drag each other down in a surreal cycle of never-ending reposts, an infinite regression of appointments and deadlines; first drafts and second drafts and third drafts of unnecessary texts being inefficiently composed by too many people at once; offers, notifications, announcements, rescheduling, FYI, reminders, your bills, your tickets, your rental car reservations, many more correspondences than you would have thought necessary about your cheese of the season club and your monthly kitty litter delivery, pictures of your sister's dessert from last night.

Depending on how methodically you prune and delete, there may well be email in your inbox from people you don't see anymore; from people you don't even remember having met; from people who once worked with you but have long since retired. I have email in my inbox from people who are, now, dead to me. And I have email from people who are actually dead. Remember how nineteenth-century telegraph users thought that electricity might bridge the gap from this world to the next? Has anyone ever tried to respond to email from someone who has shed his mortal coil? Was there any sort of reply? Something comparable to an out of office bounceback, but for eternity?

From 2015 to 2016, according to the U.S. Enterprise State of Work Report, the time office workers spent on their actual job duties dropped from 46 percent of the workday to 39 percent; it's as if a 9-to-5-er did productive work until only 12:07. Excessive emails are among the biggest obstacles to efficiency. "Workers' views of email are increasingly lukewarm, and some outrightly negative. . . . While they tout the effectiveness of email, they also blame its overuse for hurting their productivity." People report working longer hours yet getting less done. They take fewer lunch breaks, instead catching up on email at their desks.[3]

Our inboxes distract: the electronic screen is an "ecosystem of interruption technologies"[4] with its sirenlike calls to answer our email, buy something from Amazon, watch YouTube, or look something up on Google. In *The Shallows: What the Internet Is Doing to Our Brains*, Nicholas Carr argues that "we are sabotaging ourselves, trading away the seriousness of sustained attention for the frantic superficiality of the Internet."[5]

"Regaining our initial momentum following an interruption can take, on average, upwards of 20 minutes," writes Ron Friedman. We like to think of ourselves as efficient multitaskers, but we are not. "Who knows what that next email, tweet or text message holds in store? Finding out provides immediate gratification. In contrast, resisting distraction and staying on-task requires discipline and mental effort." To be effective at our jobs, Friedman advises, we must simply "muster the willpower to resist the temptations" of the inbox.[6] In order to attain *Focused Success in a Distracted World* (the title of a book by Cal Newport) we need to commit ourselves to doing "deep work":

> Knowledge workers increasingly replace deep work with the shallow alternative—constantly sending and receiving e-mail messages like human network routers, with frequent breaks for quick hits of distraction. Larger efforts that would be well served by deep thinking, such as

forming a new business strategy or writing an important grant application, get fragmented into distracted dashes that produce muted quality.[7]

"The world's workers are typing themselves into a corner," writes John Freeman.

> In some places, all you hear is the ambient hum of the central air-conditioning unit, the creak of Aeron chairs, the cricketlike click of the mouse, and the faint clatter of keystrokes. But if you lean into cubicles or peer between doorways, you will see hunched, tense figures at their computers frantically trying to keep up with their inboxes. Interrupt them, and you will find their expressions glazed, their eyes dried out and weary. Their keyboard has become a messaging conveyor belt—and there is no break time.[8]

Email is behaviorally addictive. Social psychologist Adam Alter defines such an addiction as "something you enjoy doing in the short term, that undermines your well-being in the long term—but that you do compulsively anyway." Surveys report that 60 percent of adults say they keep their cellphones next to them when they sleep, and half check their email during the night. Physician, heal thyself: Alter admits, "I'm addicted to email. I can't stop checking it. I can't go to bed at night if I haven't cleared my inbox. I'll keep my phone next to my bed, much as I try not to. The technology is designed to hook us that way. Email is bottomless."[9]

The ingress to email's egregious encroachment is the inbox. In what? Where's the box? Who puts things in? How? Why? Email's structural elements, such as the inbox, coopt terminology that connotes real physical aspects of paper and communication as they existed in the past. The nostalgic discourse suggests that we are technologically overwhelmed, even alienated (h/t Marx) and estranged from our humanity, by the hypermechanistic process of pushing keys that launch bytes of digital data through cyberspace. Instead, seeking at least some small familiar comfort in lexical archaisms, we "send" a piece of "mail" in response to a "note" that appears "in" our "inbox."

FIGURE 11 The retro physical touchstone for the inbox as object. A hovering outbox cleverly precludes an overflowing inbox. Jake Simonds-Malamud.

An inbox once sat at the corner of a desk. Secretaries put things in the busy executive's, or editor's, or middle manager's inbox. The guy behind the desk acted on it (read it, edited it, signed it, stamped it) and moved it to the outbox for filing, typing, or distribution.

The stylized inbox-as-icon emphasizes not paper or mail (nor any particular object) actually being placed into the inbox, but merely the abstracted, objectless action of *going in*.

Something goes in a box, but *what*? Not an arrow, obviously; the actual object that would go *in* the *box* is overwritten by the arrow, which is the semiotic signifier of in-going.

Anything could go in. Nothing is going in. Going in is. In is going.

The email inbox is an illusion, a metaphor, a construct. Things may be stored, arranged, dumped, *therein*, but *in* there they are not *boxed*. They are the opposite of boxed: they are boundless, they contain multitudes. The objects in your inbox will never overflow the box's edges, even if you have (as I do) over 25,000 of them.

We check our inboxes obsessively: right after we wake up and shortly before we go to sleep; immediately upon arriving at the office and as soon as we come back from lunch. Also, probably, after using the lavatory. Or even . . . (*Urban Dictionary*, "analog shit": "Having to go to the toilet without a phone. 'I left my cellphone at home; now I have to take an analog shit like a caveman.'"[10])

If we have correspondents or colleagues in London, Shanghai, or Mumbai, we make a point of checking our inbox when *they* wake up, and get to work, and get back from lunch. If the email client homepage makes a ping announcing every email, perhaps we open each one instantaneously, as soon as it "lands" in our inbox. If a correspondent responds with as much alacrity, we might have an IM-type conversation by email: ping, ping, ping.

What do you do with whatever is in your inbox? Move items into various hierarchies of folders? Print things out? Delete? Leave items there until the end of the day, for final review? Leave some unanswered (until when?) if they seem lower priority than others? Save nonwork emails for nonwork time?

Once upon a time in the eee, an inbox seemed to have some limit: a finite amount of storage that, when approached, generated warnings of some kind or slowed down your system. Culling was warranted: attention must be paid. Now technological advances make inboxes limitless. If you receive an email informing that your inbox is nearly full and you need to click on a link to resolve the problem, *you are being phished!* Chortling to yourself about how there's no moss growing on you, delete that email. Or keep it—it doesn't matter.

Yet despite (or possibly because of) this inbox infinitude, a movement called "Inbox Zero" has established a beachhead. Its puritanically fervent adherents loathe the potential for lassitude and hoarding that (they think) brews in a bottomless inbox. Books, websites, and podcasts supply copious TED-talk-like homilies about the virtues of Inbox Zero. (Spoiler, if you want to skip the sermons: simply delete everything from your inbox.)

Merlin Mann, the guru of what he calls this "Action-based email program," offers his origin story, "my own struggles over the years of dealing with high volumes of email." In 1993, his first email account

> blew my mind. I knew a dozen people who had email addresses—mostly people in grad school. I would write them letters—they would get there immediately! And then they would write me back. This was astonishing: the sense of connecting with people. It was fantastic. It was unbelievable. Every email was a special little letter. It was like I was getting a little hug from somebody. And I was returning a little hug.[11]

But within a few years, as his address book grew,

> it went from being a funny hip thing . . . into being the lingua franca for how you dealt with your entire life, and it became the one source for all incoming and outgoing information, and it started to get a lot harder, and the messages became less like careful letters, and more like an avalanche falling on your head every morning, and it became a lot less fun, and less like a network of hugs.[12]

At first, he didn't need a system. "To have a system for doing email with a network of a dozen people was silly." But today, "the only way you're going to succeed at a job, one of the most important soft skills you have to have is how to deal with a high volume of email. You have to put some kind of system into place that is simple, and repeatable, and will allow you to have some kind of a life outside email." This system must be all-encompassing, allowing you "to deal with everything that comes into your world. Reduce the number of possible options for what something could be."

Mann inveighs against people "living in their inbox. They leave it open all day long, it autochecks throughout the day, little blips come up every minute, and email becomes the nexus for everything they do at work." Quoting *The Big Lebowski's* Walter Sobchak, he warns email addicts: "'You are entering a world of pain.' That is not a way to live." Knowledge workers, people who add value to information, have two main resources, he explains: "time and attention, both finite, irreplaceable. Where you put your time and attention says a lot about who you are."

There's no need for you to live in email. That's not where the action is. Don't focus on the email to the exclusion of the things that are in the email that need to be liberated to other places. Figure out where stuff goes, where to put it. Where does stuff need to land? Figure that out. Process to zero. Every time you check your email: process, to zero. Convert stuff into action: decide, in the moment, what you need to do. . . . Think of yourself as an information miner—there are little veins of gold in your email—figure out what they are. Once you've mined the gold out of your emails, it's a dead skeletal husk, and you can throw it away.

Don't cling in this sad, Buddhist way to your email. . . .
Move it on. Get it out of your way. Get it off your plate.[13]

To get to Zero, use Mann's five-step program: 1. Delete; 2. Delegate (by forwarding the email); 3. Respond (if you can respond quickly); 4. Defer (put it aside for later); 5. If it's something you can do, go do it now and be done with it. Create an archive: just a single folder, called "archive." But don't fiddle around in your inbox—don't play with email. Don't use it as a to-do list. Don't let things sit there without a reason. Eschew clutter. Embrace action. Shut your email off sometimes and let it accumulate. "Create little email corpses as often as possible. Go off and do real work."[14]

Mann's mantra: "Don't love email."

But what if you do? Why is it so tempting to hang around here in our inboxes? We have established that there could theoretically be some good things dribbling through the tubes—what's wrong with hovering eagerly, waiting for one?

And even if you do drink the Kool-Aid and try to empty your inbox, Ian Bogost warns, "Email pruning doesn't enact work so much as it simulates work: It's a ritual—like a secular, corporate rosary—which we perform in the hopes that it will somehow help us leave the domain of ineffectual work and re-enter the domain of gratifying productivity."[15] It's a game we play with ourselves. I enjoy deleting email from colleagues I dislike when they retire. It's fun to search my inbox (and then my sent-mail) for emails from or to "Leon," and then go through and expunge all 132, one by one. I even reread a bunch of them as I was doing this, thinking of all the time I wasted exchanging email with him, and yes, admittedly, wasting a little *more* time, but glad that I would never have to again. That mole was whacked.

As I read through my inbox, detached from the context of immediacy, the contents don't age well. They mostly do not stand the test of time. They are weird to reread. They are not of much writerly interest, but they do have a significant documentary component—I can relive my life. They are like part of my brain, my memory: not so much the creative part, but the chronological part, the living part, the working, buying, lunching, meeting part.

Here is the email at the very bottom of my inbox, from my son's second-grade teacher (Ben is now 22).

```
Dear Randy,

I wanted to touch base with you about an
incident that happened this morning at
school. A student told me that Ben had been
using "code words" that really stand for
inappropriate words. For example, Ben was
telling the boys that "banana" stood for
the word penis. Yassin was also doing the
same thing. From talking with the other
students, Ben and Yassin were the two who
started this. I spoke with Ben and Yassin
and they said that they had been doing this.
I also plan on contacting Yassin's parents
as well. I wanted you to be aware of this so
```

you could speak with Ben. I know that there are changes going on at home and that maybe that might have something to do with it. I have noticed a change in Ben the past couple of weeks. I usually never have to talk to him in class. Lately, I have been having to redirect his behavior. I just wanted you to be aware of that small change.

I will not be zeroing out my inbox.

9 CC/BCC

cc means (or meant) carbon copy. A sheet of crinkly paper with a blue/black powder—dry ink—on one side is placed between two sheets of letter paper. Ralph Wedgwood, of the prissy-precious pottery family, patented the invention he called "carbonated paper" in 1806.

Line up the three sheets very precisely and feed them behind the platen. "Platen": part of the carriage, which, along with the carriage return and the margin bell (the contraption's most satisfying design element!), made you feel as if you were physically making an object: crafting it, rolling it, *composing* it. These devices kept your hands busy and active while your fingers were qwerty'ing. You got a nice quick muscle stretch every twenty seconds—a platenic (Platonic?) pause, a palette cleanser—before you composed the next eighty characters. Ding! Back in platen-times people didn't get carpal tunnel syndrome nearly as often as today. And they didn't hate writing, or receiving, or reading letters. Yes, if something has been lost, *cherchez le platen*.

Papered up, the carbon copier begins to type. If residual carbon flaked off, which happened not infrequently, your shirt was ruined. The typewriter ribbon left its marks on the original (top) copy, and the keys' impression produced a second copy of the letter. That is, it worked if you struck the keyboard with sufficient pressure that the mark of the typebar's imprint passed through the ribbon, the original letter paper, the carbon paper, and then all the way through to the copy. If the carbon copies were fuzzy, you'd need to use a little more muscle.

The cc was to save for your files; photocopy machines were not yet a thing. A mistake on the top copy could be corrected with Wite-Out (or, before that was invented, hard rubber typewriter erasers), but the carbon copy indelibly bore the marks of errata, sticky keys, and overstrikes. People mostly weren't bothered by the cc's textual imperfections: it was good enough.

The typist could even add a second piece of carbon paper, followed by a third piece of letter paper, to produce a second cc; conceivably even a third carbon and a fourth letter could be inserted (there's a gizmo for allowing a bit more space around the platen to accommodate all these sheafs): but this would require an extremely fierce, almost superhuman, intensity of percussion.

Making more than one copy of something required a special effort, a special intent. A cc'd email, on the other hand, is easy to create: probably way too easy. A common complaint about email distribution is that too many people receive too many cc's of things they don't need to read. You *might* want to read an email (and reply?) on which you have been cc'd, or you might not.

And then there's the bcc—the "blind carbon copy," a concept that would have been inconceivable to Wedgwood. The recipient does not know you have been sent this, nor do others who have been cc'd. Secrecy, intrigue, strategy come into play here. You know, but they do not know you know . . . maybe a whole group of people knows, but you do not know they know, and you cannot email them to ask if they know, because you do not know who they are; you, too, are blinded. (NB: In the unfortunate event that your emails are FOIA'd—that is, requested by a member of the public under the Freedom of Information Act—everyone will know everything: the blindness will be lifted as if your email had made a pilgrimage to Lourdes.) "In some cases," Wikipedia opines, "use of Blind Carbon Copy may be viewed as mildly unethical. The original addressee of the mail is left under the impression that communication is proceeding between the known parties, and is knowingly kept unaware of others participating in the primary communication."[1]

The bcc recalls other epistolary subterfuges: invisible ink, cryptographic codes and ciphers; switched letters (Rosencrantz and Guildenstern); mask letters (the recipient placed a shaped template over the full letter, whose true message would then appear within the boundaries of the "mask," which was delivered by a separate courier to ensure secrecy); hidden letters (rolled up in a feather's hollowed-out quill, or even folded into a button).

You learn stuff when you study email. There's a history, a technological tradition, lurking beneath the surface, however evanescent that tradition seems, however much it has been overwritten. Platens, bells, carbon copies, and so on, are objects that email has dispatched: rationalized, streamlined.

No doubt the resulting technology is cheaper and more efficient: no smudges. But also, no doubt, a corpus of significant materiality has evaporated along with these superannuated objects. While we have established that email is not absolutely objectless, still, its quotient of objects has been reduced, diminished: many would argue, sadly diminished. It has been shorn of the bells and carriage returns, quills and wax and philatelic frippery, that used to connect the writers to the written texts, which profusely bore the marks of our own imprint. *We* folded the letters, and put them in the envelopes. We might even SWAK the envelopes, the objects: with our lipstick, our lips, our saliva, our perfume, our love. While every song about email is bad, songs about actual letters tend to be pretty good. SWAK ("sealed with a kiss") cues up a soundtrack-of-the-mind featuring Bryan Hyland's 1962 much-improved cover of the Four Voices' lugubrious 1960 original, also pleasantly sung by Bobby Vinton (1964), Gary Lewis & the Playboys (1968) and Jason Donovan (1989). Feel free to sing along—I defy you *not* to: "Though we've got to say goodbye for the summer / Darling, I promise you this / I'll send you all my love, every day in a letter / Sealed with a kiss."

But epistolary emotions have been reduced and stylized into "emojis." It may be technically, graphically, possible to smooch an email but why even bother?

FIGURE 12 A kiss is just a kiss. www.symbols-n-emoticons.com.

The trappings of letters have been stripped away in a process that leaves merely pure text. Our precious bodily fluids (recalling, again, *Dr. Strangelove*), including our actual DNA, used to be component objects comprising our mail: along with SWAK-spit, letters included two other pools of saliva: stamp-slobber and envelope-sealing-drool were part and parcel of these parcels. This new and improved phenomenon of email, though not without its own objectness, is profoundly distanced from our pencils, our hands, our sensory connections to the correspondence, our lips and tongues and fluids; it is hidden away behind (or inside) the codes, the tubes, the passwords, the bulking inboxes. When we finally get a fix on this email object, fair warning, we will find it less graspable, less meaningful, less durable, less interesting, less human than the many cognate objects that have been disambiguated and discarded on the path to its existence. A simulacrum of mail, email resembles its precursor to a considerably more paltry degree than an old-fashioned cc resembled the original letter.

10 PRINT

Don't print. C'mon—that's the point of email. Save a tree. This is, seriously, its main selling point: this is how email will save the world. You don't have to print! It's *there*. In your inbox.

When late-twentieth-century businesses began using email, Abigail Sellen and Richard Harper write in *The Myth of the Paperless Office*, paper consumption increased by 40 percent.[1] *facepalm*

Email encourages us to take the intention for the deed: we cling to the virtuous illusion of (theoretical, not actual) paperlessness, and we preen with the placatory pretense that it is a sustainable technology.

It's not . . . and the wasted paper is the least of it.

Sending and storing email requires gargantuan data centers (there are over eight million[2]), fortresslike dynamos that consume massive amounts of energy, specifically *electricity*—which, my perspicacious reader will have already observed, is literally in the word "email," making it pretty disingenuous to pretend that sending paperless spreadsheets around the planet is carbon-neutral. Despite

FIGURE 13 Google Data Center, The Dalles, Oregon. Creative Commons Attribution-Share Alike 3.0 Unported License.

its airy aura, we might reasonably characterize email as a object comprised of a calculable quantity of kilowatt-hours, plant emissions, diesel exhaust, lead-acid battery seepage, and even, if you want to be ecologically woke about it, polar bear corpses: the world warms as our inboxes churn, melting the ice floes where the bears live(d).

Print, don't print . . . I guess it's a lost cause anyway.

11 FORWARD

"The ease with which an email can be forwarded poses a danger."[1]

12 OUT OF OFFICE

In the eee, being out of office meant that a person actually wouldn't have access to her email (no computer, no tubes), so would be unable to monitor her inbox for a certain period of time, a fact conveyed concisely in an automatic response: the "out of office email." If Ayesha down the hall might pitch in during the hiatus, this too would be noted.

Today it is virtually inconceivable that anyone could be so far off the grid as to be out of email contact. Airports and airplanes have wifi, as do hotels, McDonald's and Starbucks, cruise ships, public libraries, hospitals, malls, parks, museums; even other people's routers have become hotspots. There are no excuses for not checking your email. You can run, but you can't hide.

So now, the point is not that I *cannot* respond, but rather, in the spirit of Bartleby, I would prefer not to. The masterpieces of this genre invoke literary color, philosophy, memoir, humor, empathy, in the hopes of inducing the indulgent correspondent to grant a temporary respite from the hamster-wheel of email. Viz:

Today I travel, if fortune be fair; I am armed with Virtue; I shall make the Journeye from Tampa to Charlotte and then, anon, to Washington National. Neither Ice nor Wynd shall delay me, and I shall not be waylaid by Ruffians. I may not see your Emaile, however, until Tomorrow.

I am currently on vacation and not accepting any emails about anything. I'm not planning on reading any old emails when I get back, either, because that feels antithetical to the vacation experience.

I want you to imagine a middle-aged man who fell in love with a beautiful baby girl almost 18 years ago, and now he is driving her to a gigantic college in a distant city filled with all kinds of people who do the things people do at college . . . and he has to leave her there. And drive home alone. In the dark. In a minivan.[1]

High anxiety about what the world will think when you do not immediately answer your email surfaces in a plethora of advice on how to tell business contacts you've gone fishin'. *Forbes* offers some high-octane suggestions in an article headlined "What Successful People Say in Out of Office Email," advising that the absentee might alleviate the absence by providing a link to an article, letting others know about a recent accomplishment, or giving a sneak peek of what's on tap: "use the out of office email to let people know what you will be doing, whether it is an upcoming project, partnership or speaking engagement. Give people a good excuse to circle back when you return to engage you in a meaningful way."[2]

Here's mine:

I am on leave for the Fall semester; I am unable to respond to your email because I am writing a book on email (called *Email*). You could think of my forthcoming book as a macrocosmic response to your email . . . or not. But, you might persist, how about just a quick response, simply yes or no, up or down, in or out? Sent at a time most convenient for you, a few days is ok, I don't mind waiting, when it wouldn't interrupt your writing? Really, I hate to close down this imaginary conversation but oddly, I have found that I cannot write email while I am writing *Email*. It's a paradox; perhaps even an affectation. I have a lot of complicated thoughts about this, which you will appreciate better if you read *Email*.

13 OPT OUT

- Julian Assange: "I don't use email. . . . Too dangerous. And encrypted email is possibly even worse, because it is such a flag for end point attacks."[1]

- Senator Lindsey Graham: "I don't email, no. You can have every email I've ever sent. I've never sent one. . . . I've tried not to have a system where I can just say the first dumb thing that comes to my mind. . . . I'm trying to jealously guard myself in terms of being able to think through problems and not engage in chat all day. I've had a chance to kind of carve out some time for myself not responding to every 15-second crisis."[2]

- Senator John McCain: "I don't email at all. I have other people and I tell them to email because I am just always worried I might say something. I am not the most calm and reserved person you know? I am afraid I might email something that in retrospect I wish I hadn't."[3]

- Most of the U.S. Supreme Court: One of its youngsters, Elena Kagan, says the other justices write memos printed on ivory paper that looks like it came from the nineteenth century and is walked around the building by someone called a "chambers aide." The justices "are not necessarily the most technologically sophisticated people," Kagan said; "The court hasn't really 'gotten to' email."[4]

- Millennials: Texting, Snapchat, Instagram, Finstagram, Facebook, Twitter, Tinder, emojis, tattoos. ~~Email.~~

- New York Attorney General Eliot Spitzer: "Never talk when you can nod. And never write when you can talk. Never put it in an email."[5]

- Umberto Eco: "I don't even have an e-mail address. I have reached an age where my main purpose is not to receive messages."[6]

- Head honchos: "Not using email, or having a team of people to deal with your email for you, is a way of reasserting hierarchy, and it's not that different from the situation of 30 years ago where senior professionals would have a team of secretaries screening their memos," says James Crabtree from the iSociety project, which examines technology's impact in the workplace. "Some people say that they don't use email as a status thing. Some don't have to because they have a pool of people answering emails for them. Then, of course, there are plenty who don't use it because they don't know how to."[7]

- Donald Trump: "I'm not an email person myself. I don't believe in it," he said. "I think it can be hacked, for one thing. When I send an email, I mean, if I send one, I send one almost never. I'm just not a believer in email. A lot of people have taught me that, including Hillary. But, honestly, it could be maybe attacked. Who knows."[8] He advises: "You know, if you have something really important, write it out and have it delivered by courier, the old-fashioned way. Because I'll tell you what: No computer is safe."[9]

- Stanford computer scientist Donald Knuth: "I have been a happy man ever since January 1, 1990, when I no longer had an email address. I'd used email since about 1975, and it seems to me that 15 years of email is plenty for one lifetime. Email is a wonderful thing for people whose role in life is to be on top of things. But not for me; my role is to be on the bottom of things. What I do takes long hours of studying and uninterruptible concentration."[10]

- Christopher Nolan: "I've never used email because I don't find it would help me with anything I'm doing."[11]

- French people (*dans la nuit*): a 2017 labor law enshrined "the right to disconnect," giving employees the right not to reply to email between 9:00 p.m. and 7:00 a.m. The idea is to preserve nonwork time from office spillover. As a news headline puts it, "France Lets Workers Turn Off, Tune Out and Live Life."[12]

- In Germany, "Daimler has a program that automatically deletes all incoming work emails during an employee's vacation, and lets the sender know they should contact someone else."[13]

- University of Michigan administrators suggest curbing after-hours email: "We're not saying you can't write emails at night. . . . You just wouldn't send them." Colleagues "were swimming in email . . . spending hours every evening dealing with messages that had come in over the course of the day. . . . The blurred line between work and personal time" makes their workplace less appealing: "we all needed sustained, significant, meaningful time away from administrative work." Even if the evening emailer, clearing out her inbox's day-residue, doesn't necessarily expect an immediate answer, still the recipient may feel compelled to respond right away and the cycle accelerates. "Very few issues cannot wait until morning. . . . Problems often resolve themselves when they're left alone for a little while."[14]

Could it be that *the magic of email*—instantaneous, ubiquitous, 24/7—is also its *curse*? That what's so brilliant about it is also what sucks about it? As the fable of King Midas suggests, be careful what you wish for.

- One more opter-outer (until, unluckily, she opted in): Hillary Clinton. "I didn't send a single email while I was in the White House as First Lady or during most of my first term in the U.S. Senate. I've never used a computer at home or at work. It was not until about 2006 that I began sending and receiving emails on a BlackBerry phone."[15] And thereby hangs a tale.

14 DELETE

An email that has been read and acted upon—its lifeblood sucked dry—could sensibly be deleted. Dispatch it to make it your inbox more manageable. As Monty Python might say: This email is no more. It has ceased to be. It's expired and gone to meet its maker! It's a stiff! THIS IS AN EX-EMAIL!!

Deleted email is still sometimes, somehow, possibly recoverable, in some server or cloud, or via some subpoena, or leaker, or hacker. Maybe the delete key is a placebo, a programmer's inside joke. I think puncturing the hard drive with a drill might fundamentally delete and destroy the email (I saw this in a movie), but I am not sure.

There is no reason to expect that a deleted email will come back, zombielike, years past its sell-by date. (*Nobody* expects the Spanish Inquisition!)

"Lock her up," chanted presidential candidate Donald Trump, and the crowds parroted back his threat like a frenzied team chant. Hillary Clinton stood accused of having sent and deleted—or, possibly, *not* deleted—email from her term as Secretary of State: inappropriately, deviously, seditiously, sloppily, unprofessionally, undiplomatically, irresponsibly. The pedestrian details of her email habits percolated during the 2016 campaign into a referendum on her trustworthiness and her very fitness to serve as Commander in Chief: it was arguably the campaign's determinative issue. Trump sowed doubt about his opponent's electability with such Tweets as:

> How can Hillary run the economy when she can't even send emails without putting entire nation at risk?

> One of the reasons Hillary hid her emails was so the public wouldn't see how she got rich—selling out America.

> Voters understand that Crooked Hillary's negative ads are not true—just like her email lies and her other fraudulent activity.[1]

Investigating a possible breach of the 1917 Espionage Act, which punishes anyone who imperils classified national defense information through gross negligence, the FBI found hdr22@clintonemail.com innocent . . . but also, sort of culpable . . . careless but not criminal . . . but then some more emails turned up on Anthony Weiner's computer on October 28 . . . or wait, maybe they were the same ones? Clinton later declared, "If the election had been on October 27, I would be your president."[2]

"Lock her up" became a platform, a meme, even a Halloween costume, that embodied the misogynistic bullying invoked upon this "crooked" woman who had the temerity to run for president. Clinton's email transgression, whatever that might have been, opened the floodgates for all the fear and hatred that her campaign evoked.

Trump accused Clinton of "acid washing" the emails; in fact, she used a free software application, BleachBit, to delete and destroy 32,000 emails she characterized as personal, after submitting 31,000 work-related emails to the State Department in 2015.[3] (To contextualize those numbers, the George W. Bush administration produced 200 million emails—and lost some 22 million of them[4]—while the Obama White House generated about 300 million.[5]) Trump famously invited foreign hackers to find and restore Clinton's deleted emails—"Russia, if you're listening, I hope you're able to find the 30,000 emails that are missing"[6]—which, apparently, they did, that very day.[7]

Secretary Clinton used her own private server rather than an official government email account "as a matter of convenience," FBI Director James Comey concluded. She apologized, took responsibility for the lapse, called it "a dumb mistake."[8] As people of a certain age are prone to do, she pleaded incompetence:

> A lot of young people today are used to carrying around multiple devices and having both a personal phone and one provided by their work. But I'm not a digital native. (I couldn't even have told you what that term meant until fairly recently.) . . . Adding another email account when I became Secretary of State would have meant juggling a second phone.[9]

The content of the email cache is much less interesting
than the campaign rhetoric it unleashed. Perusing the
WikiLeaks Hillary Clinton Email Archive, we learn that she
is often referred to by others, and by herself, as H. Also,
sometimes, Madame. She made a lot of typos. She sent and
received many articles about foreign policy and about her
own diplomatic and media presence. "Info for u" and "H:
MUST READ WHEN YOU CAN" are copiously recurring
subject lines, as are "PLS PRINT" and "can u print pls."
(Disappointingly, she does not seem all that concerned
about conserving paper.) There is an immense amount of
bureaucratic organizational tedium steeping in this corpus.
Possibly a few of her emails could be of some interest to
some scholar on some topic of American politics, but
mostly they are morsels like this:

```
From: H
Sent: Monday, February 20, 2012 11:31 AM
To: Huma Abedin
Subject: I'm venting

So, here I sit in the meeting surrounded
by every other person dressed in a white
shirt provided by the Mexicans. Patricia is
not wearing the exact style that all others
are but her own white shirt. But, since no
one ever told me about this, and instead
assumed I didn't need to know, I had no idea
about any of this until I just walked into
```

the large meeting in front of the entire press corps and am wearing a green top. So, what's my answer when asked why I think I'm different than all my colleagues and why I'm dissing our hosts? I am sick of people deciding what I should know rather than giving me the info so I can make a decision. This really annoys me and I told Monica I just didn't understand what she/they were doing. But, when we do the family photo, I will be the only person not in white.

The response:

From: Huma Abedin
Sent: Monday, February 20, 2012 01:34 PM
To: H
Subject: Re: I'm venting

This is awful. I'm so sorry. They should have showed it to you. We didn't find out about the need to wear shirt till you got to mexico. They sent me a picture and I said I hoped you didn't wear it cause it looked quite unattractive! but assumed they would discuss it with you. I should have confirmed they did. I will take responsibility and I am so so sorry. We will move forward with people knowing to tell you everything!

Subject, "Tipper's father died" generates H's response, "Pls do letter." Subject, "Judy's mom" generates "Pls draft condolence note for me. Thx." And then there's this inscrutable enigma:

```
From: Hillary Clinton
To: Richard Verma
Date: 2010-03-04 02:56
Subject: GEFILTE FISH

Where are we on this?[10]
```

Why were there so many emails, so many vacuous emails? (Have you been *reading* my book so far? Welcome to email.) An aide destroyed two of her thirteen private BlackBerries with a hammer,[11] but this seems to have been a day late and a dollar short. Is deleting email unpresidential? Is keeping them? I said at the outset that there will never be an interesting or important email. Let me modify that: An email is important only when it goes wrong. Even if email is banal and pointless, still, you can be held responsible for it. Don't get cocky; don't forget that it has danger lurking within it. There are so many emails that one of them is bound to be, not *King Lear*, but incriminating; unfortunate.

"A lot of people still don't understand what it was all about; they just know it was bad," Clinton writes in *What Happened* (in a chapter entitled "Those Damn Emails"). "And I can't blame them: they were told that over and over for a year and a half. For most of the general election campaign, the word *email* dominated all others when people were asked to name the first word that came to mind about me."[12]

Clinton was judged and defeated based not on her actual email, not on email as an object in any sense, but on an idea of email, a Trumped-up misrepresentation of email that was as ridiculous as his misrepresentations of Mexican rapists and Obama's birth certificate. The 2016 electorate, whose intelligence no one went broke underestimating, was left with a sense that email had gotten the better of Clinton: that she had lost control of her email (which is on some level a battle we all fight every day, trying to keep our heads above water as we bilge-pump out our inboxes) and if she couldn't do *that*, well then, how could she run the country? Even as she struggles in her book to put paid to this issue, we can only imagine the unbearable irony she must feel from the realization that Trump's America—sexual predation, unending racist vitriol, bottomless sleaze, diplomatic anarchy, melting icecaps, insanely inept and immoral leadership, probably treason, the swamp to end all swamps, the lies to end all lies—was the consequence of her imperfect email protocol.

Right off the bat, let me say that, yes, the decision to use personal email instead of an official government account was mine and mine alone. I own that. I never meant to mislead anyone, never kept my email use secret, and always took classified information seriously. During the campaign, I tried endlessly to explain that I'd acted in good faith. I tried to apologize, though I knew the attacks being lobbed at me were untrue or wildly overstated, and motivated by partisan politics. Sometimes I dove deep into the tedious details. Other times I tried to rise above it all. Once I even told a bad joke. No matter what, I never found the right words. So let me try again: It was a dumb mistake. But an even dumber scandal. It was like quicksand: the more you struggle, the deeper you sink.[13]

The joke: "When asked by reporters if her server had been wiped, the leading Democratic presidential candidate Hillary Clinton shot back: 'What, like with a cloth or something?' She then proceeded not to answer the question."[14]

15 JUNK

Now along comes *Email* (but IT IS NOT AN EMAIL! It is A BOOK that just happens to be called *Email!*) that will reinvigorate your existence. You will write better emails— but only if you read every word, including, especially, the INSIGHTS that await you at the END. You will acquire a sense of history and context that will empower you to understand, and make peace with, the process and product of email. You will learn to appreciate what there is to appreciate in the miracle of electronic communication, and you will let the rest go. You will laugh, and you will cry. You will take charge. You will not let your inbox trample your spirit as if you were a pathetic little wimp, or rule your life like a deranged dominatrix.

You will become wryly meta: from this moment forth, every email you send or receive from your phone, laptop, desktop, or smartwatch, from your own fingers ("thumbs") or as dictated via Siri or Alexa, will be enriched by the astonishing stories and lessons, cognitive and creative, sociological and philosophical, intellectual and ethical, contained herein. To you will be revealed a sense of semiotic depth, a textual *je ne sais quoi*, that will elevate your e-life far above the hue and cry of the mobs who catapult their incessant trivialities into your inbox.

You will become an ironically detached *flâneur* of the cyberarcades. Away from the hurly-burly, far from the madding crowds, you will find yourself positioned as at the towering eye of a panopticon where you may monitor the madness. Respond to your email, or don't respond: you decide. Here is the thread sticking out just so from the fabric of cyberspace: yank it with glee and watch the whole blooming edifice unravel, leaving you free to recalibrate and reconceptualize whom you communicate with and when, and how. Turn your lemons into lemonade. Beat your swords into plowshares.

Learn the HIDDEN SECRETS of what email really is. Where it came from. Where it is going. How YOU CAN MASTER the textual effluvia flowing in and out of your computer.

Read on. You have nothing to lose but your chains.

Please forward this book to ten friends.

16 DELIVERY FAILURE

In Oslo once, I got this wonderfully bizarre note accompanying a bounced-back email:

Error 503 Backend is unhealthy

Backend is unhealthy

Guru Meditation:

Details: cache bma7031-BMA 1484377417 842691337

Varnish cache server

I wondered if "Backend is unhealthy" was a Google-translated version of "pain in the ass"? Perhaps someone in the Norwegian Department of Errors has a sense of humor. Looking up Error 503, I learned: "Varnish, the software that powers the Fastly CDN, will sometimes return standardized 503 responses due to various issues that can occur when attempting to fetch data from your origin servers. The generic status text associated with a 503 error is 'Service Unavailable.' It can mean a wide variety of things."[1]

I like that: *It can mean a wide variety of things*. I think most recipients of such error notices would flinch in derision if their email servers frolicked in such polyvalent perversity, indeterminacy, evasion, *jouissance*. But Norse folk are made of sterner stuff, and their Scandinavian strain of *hygge*-zen apparently invites a Guru Meditation on email delivery failure. ("The Guru Meditation is an error notice displayed by early versions of the Commodore Amiga computer when they crashed. It is analogous to the 'Blue Screen of Death' in Microsoft Windows operating systems, or a kernel panic in Unix."[2]) *Uff da*.

Back in the US of A, as part of my research for this book, I was anthropologically parsing my own electronic epistles and sent an email to a very old friend, a high school pal whose last note to me was lurking near the bottom of my inbox. I didn't think Bob would still be at that *fin de siècle* email address, and indeed he wasn't, as an email I received a week later informed:

```
Delivery has failed to these recipients or
groups:

robertslate@gobi.com     (robertslate@gobi.
com). Your message wasn't delivered. Despite
repeated attempts to deliver your message,
the recipient's email system refused to
accept a connection from your email system.
```

Contact the recipient by some other means
(by phone, for example) and ask them to
tell their email admin that it appears that
their email system is refusing connections
from your email server. Give them the error
details shown below. It's likely that the
recipient's email admin is the only one who
can fix this problem.

The technical term for this email is "NDR": Non-Delivery Report. Please mister postman, cue the Marvelettes: "Please check and see just one more time for me. . . . Deliver the letter the sooner the better." Elvis, too, provides a soundtrack for a return-to-sender: "We had a quarrel, a lover's spat / I write I'm sorry but my letter keeps coming back."[3] (It's not just me, is it? These really *are* objectively better songs than "Bye bye baby, please check your email," or "Send me an email, tell me how you're doing," right?)

The tenor of the NDR mildly evokes the tireless mailman's motto: "despite repeated attempts. . . ." We try hard too! Neither snow nor rain nor heat nor gloom of night prevents the electronic circuits and IMAP and SMTP from completing their rounds. There's also a hint of defensiveness: not our fault!

I let out a sharp guffaw when they advise: "Contact the recipient by some other means (by phone, for example)." Thank you, email, for reminding me what "some other means" of contacting people are. Yeah, I don't have Bob's phone number. I don't save phone numbers anymore because you lulled me into thinking that email was eternal and infallible.

The NDR message isn't extremely helpful or soothing, but . . . it is what it is: the system failed; the email failed. This doesn't happen often, but it is clearly in the realm of possibility. In the olden days, a sender could put a trace on a letter that did not find its recipient: people would spring into action to investigate the snafu. There was an actual place, a dead letter office—London's first such institution opened in 1784—to coordinate this rescue mission. (Herman Melville's Bartleby used to work as a dead letter officer, rumor had it, before he became a scrivener.) If an address was indeterminate, a dead letter officer might open the waylaid letter for clues about where it was meant to go.

Were my NDR administrators so diligent, I wonder? Their report links to a page with much information about Error Codes and Sender Policy Framework (SPF) records and Hybrid Deployment Configuration issues, but basically what they're trying to tell me is, I'm screwed. It's not gonna happen. DNR the NDR. As hard as it is to believe, sometimes the tubes go awry.

The best part of the NDR (and it took me several days of staring at this to notice what a gem was buried here), an initially indecipherable smorgasbord of gobbledygook at the bottom, embodies a surprisingly revelatory look behind the scenes of email:

Diagnostic information for administrators:

Generating server: DM5PR05MB3147.namprd05.
prod.outlook.com

Receiving server: DM5PR05MB3147.namprd05.
prod.outlook.com

robertslate@gobi.com

11/19/2017 2:26:39 PM - Server at DM5PR05MB
3147.namprd05.prod.outlook.com returned '550
5.4.316 Message expired, connection refused
(Socket error code 10061)'

11/19/2017 2:16:10 PM - Server at gobi.
com (199.106.109.198) returned '450 4.4.316
Connection refused [Message=Socket error
code 10061] [LastAttemptedServerName=gobi.
com] [LastAttemptedIP=199.106.109.198:25]
[SN1NAM01FT012.eop-nam01.prod.protection.
outlook.com](Socket error code 10061)'

Original message headers:

DKIM-Signature:v=1;a=rsa-sha256;c=relaxed/
relaxed; d=mygsu.onmicrosoft.com;

s=selector1-gsu-edu;

h=From:Date:Subject:Message-ID:Content-
Type:MIME-Version;

bh=+Ci0/M9hb1k4ytdGoCTmvJwl1tyAcQ54d98p6
dgfjc8=;

b=czuRYTo5SIUYllQqHQr/rlLiE22EoZf0BNw0kJ
J8bKhY4+fins7DL7BWI+8mnA0r9gVPcooVMudu4+
3QFVItR+hXUFgm9xteNmNVRwgg0cGvRQhdglVaBD
e+fIj8UVzJLBNgUzy2K5gVDgbyHB4HDHDzhkiYAl
JIg/jhFV+FcTg=

Received: from DM5PR05MB3148.namprd05.
prod.outlook.com (10.173.219.18) by

DM5PR05MB3147.namprd05.prod.outlook.com
(10.173.219.17) with Microsoft SMTP

Server (version=TLS1_2, cipher=TLS_ECDHE_
RSA_WITH_AES_256_CBC_SHA384_P256) id

15.20.260.2; Fri, 17 Nov 2017 14:26:26 +0000

Received: from DM5PR05MB3148.namprd05.prod.
outlook.com ([10.173.219.18]) by

DM5PR05MB3148.namprd05.prod.outlook.com
([10.173.219.18]) with mapi id

15.20.0260.001; Fri, 17 Nov 2017 14:26:26 +0000

From: Randy Malamud <rmalamud@gsu.edu>

To: "robertslate@gobi.com" <robertslate@
gobi.com>

Subject: You still there?

Thread-Topic: You still there?

Thread-Index: AQHTX7ANTKAj3eYfAEe408J7Fta
FBQ==

Date: Fri, 17 Nov 2017 14:26:26 +0000

Message-ID: <D6345BBB.2DA64%rmalamud@gsu.
edu>

Accept-Language: en-US

Content-Language: en-US

X-MS-Has-Attach:

X-MS-TNEF-Correlator:

user-agent:Microsoft-MacOutlook/14.7.7.170905

x-ms-publictraffictype: Email

x-microsoft-exchange-diagnostics: 1;DM5
PR05MB3147;6:IYhJ/LHeV+jo6sKxu0GiF+mFaql
TAoz4a18xlzAy6hu5W6NeWdvonxIi+xnAMhyhU1n
Sp+uCCtIw9sI1jbej8fDapW0VA5H1kZSLg7LcjfS
Oo5uA5o8rOgq8YR2A26ArEgpyi4gqaEqoXTo1kEx
wL0kivPVYi2OysmIeQmIBArobXsTGv1Fuu22+X6G
K7DpFICpDfXffZF+lVU9Fc1rIa446HYkHe+ql2Et
6vRgGd7gS8fvI/fpKnq8KOXbqFiANTA2Hh4qcw3r
I7GCcqap1zLeGFbHuQS3idPUSVgTbOXfOOBruLUu
5lzOf8Etk+vYTJTGutr4PWWv5FFXTWo2+odWM3pO
sBp0c1dUxq/IekCg=;5:

x-ms-exchange-antispam-srfa-diagnostics: SSOS;

x-ms-office365-filtering-correlation-id:
b2d43034-021f-40be-9ba6-08d52dc72fb6

x-microsoft-antispam:UriScan:;BCL:0;PCL:0;
RULEID:(22001)(4534020)(4602075)(4627115)
(201703031133081)(201702281549075)(201
7052603258);SRVR:DM5PR05MB3147;

X-MS-TrafficTypeDiagnostic:DM5PR05MB3147:|
DM5PR05MB3147:

authentication-results: spf=none (sender IP is)
smtp.mailfrom=rmalamud@gsu.edu;

x-microsoft-antispam-prvs: <DM5PR05MB31476B
2D9B6DEA746A69CACCCE2F0@DM5PR05MB3147.na
mprd05.prod.outlook.com>

x-exchange-antispam-report-test: UriScan:;

x-exchange-antispam-report-cfa-test:

x-forefront-prvs: 049486C505

x-forefront-antispam-report:

LANG:en;

received-spf: None (protection.outlook.
com: gsu.edu does not designate

permitted sender hosts)

spamdiagnosticoutput: 1:99

spamdiagnosticmetadata: NSPM

Content-Type: multipart/alternative;
   boundary="_000_D6345BBB2DA64rmalamudgsue
   du_"

MIME-Version: 1.0

X-MS-Exchange-CrossTenant-Network-Message-
Id: b2d43034-021f-40be-9ba6-08d52dc72fb6

X-MS-Exchange-CrossTenant-originalarriva
ltime: 17 Nov 2017 14:26:26.4094

(UTC)

X-MS-Exchange-CrossTenant-fromentityheader:
Hosted

X-MS-Exchange-CrossTenant-id: 515ad73d-8d5e-
4169-895c-9789dc742a70

X-Microsoft-Exchange-Diagnostics: 1;DM5PR05M
B3147;23:CNJVl1Mz8zPmE9cB3ICZRUVNokHSTly
96EPujXgXxSEH/13LpASW0mAMJwks

X-OriginatorOrg: gsu.edu

Imagine that you are in what you think is an uninhabited office block, wandering down a long, quiet, dimly lit hallway in the middle of the night, and then suddenly a door opens, and you hear, for just a moment, a deafening cacophony of unruly subhuman (or suprahuman?) grunts and snorts, flashing lights and clackity mechanical spasms, armies of overcaffeinated functionaries fueled by their rage against the machine . . . or, perhaps, rage *for* the machine.

It is a primal screed, a babel of code and symbols, letters and numerals, words and near-words and abbreviations: nonrandom randomness.

This mishmash asks to be ignored; it dares you to read it. But I could not turn away, for I have concluded that this is, at root, the object lesson. We learn the lesson, we see the object for what it is, in its totality, warts and all, only when it lets down its guard: when it fails, when it misfires, when it dies. But there is no dead letter office for email; instead, it just comes back to me. I am the dead letter office. I am Bartleby. I would prefer not to. But I will: I will plunge into this bombast, this object, and find inside it the core of meaning—the essence of email. (*The e-ssence of e-mail*, I would have written, if email hadn't been disenhyphenated by my editor.)

But is it art? (Is it email art?)

It took me quite some time—your tax dollars at work!— to decipher this NDR, to let it speak to me; to de- and re-construct it, or de- and re-compose it. But my training as an English professor means that I can read texts, however difficult they might be, and read them well: I can find meaning, ethos, pattern, revelation. And I persevere. I have read *Finnegans Wake*; I have read *The Satanic Verses*; I have read *Nightwood*. You can't shake me off that easily with a veneer of gibberish.

The terms embedded in this object comprise a found poem worthy of the Dadaists or William Burroughs: It is a poem (which is to say, I will render it a poem) about barking orders, carrying things, many things, from many places to many other places, according to a protocol that is opaque, incoherent, but also accurate, methodical, even technically brilliant, proven over time to be 99.99 percent efficient.

The "poem" includes words—real words, fused words, abbreviated words, highly technical words—and sometimes, when things get crazily ecstatic, the text takes flight, mixed-numeric-alphabetic-symbolic-strings, the music of the spheres, inspired dithyrambic ecstasy like

```
IYhJ/LHeV+jo6sKxu0GiF+mFaqlTAoz4a18xlzAy
6hu5W6NeWdvonxIi+xnAMhyhU1nSp+uCCtIw9sI1
jbej8fDapW0VA5H1kZSLg7LcjfSOo5uA5o8rOgq8
YR2A26ArEgpyi4gqaEqoXTo1kExwL0kivPVYi2Oy
smIeQmIBArobXsTGv1Fuu22+X6GK7DpFICpDfXff
ZF+lVU9Fc1rIa446HYkHe+ql2Et6vRgGd7gS8fvI/
fpKnq8KOXbqFiANTA2Hh4qcw3rI7GCcqap1zLeG
FbHuQS3idPUSVgTbOXfOOBruLUu5lzOf8Etk+vYT
JTGutr4PWWv5FFXTWo2+odWM3pOsBp0c1dUxq
```

I teach my students always to read poetry aloud, to hear its innate music and rhythm. Please intone the extract above; I will wait.

IYhJ suggests an email approximation of the invocation of God: YHWH, in prEmail. LHeV is like "levitate," with extra aspiration, "H," thrown in for effect. IYhJ/LHeV connotes the divine apotheosis, the rising and overarching infinitude of what we now call, in e-speak, "the cloud."

W0VA5H: Make the "5" into an "S" for "Woe-vash." Egpyi4: Egg-pie four. These are strange and silly words, but nevertheless fun. It's not hurting anyone. What else do you have to do?

IBArobX is a keen clue: "I be a Rob—NOT!" Remember, my friend was Bob, not Rob. FiANTA sounds just as you would imagine. OXfOOB—try to keep a straight face here.

And so forth. Pick your favorite sound (mine is definitely OXfOOB), and think of it as a kind of email-era chant, the cyberversion of a meditative mantra, or a *hwyl* (a Welsh spiritual expression that invokes stirring emotional energy), or *yoik* (a shamanistic song of the earth shared by Nordic Sami cultures, given to them by fairies and elves).

I'm kidding . . . mostly: one is not expected—perhaps not even allowed—to read, or chant, or analyze and aestheticize this code. Really, it is fairly subversive even to attempt to decode this code, let alone (as I am doing here) mock-decoding, or Rorschachian decoding. (What does the code mean *to me*?) Leave it be—what you don't know can't hurt you. Ignorance is bliss. Better minds than mine. . . . The rest is silence.

But this activity, this game I am playing out here, pierces through the thickets and brings us close to the source of things. The blueprint: the skeleton: the ur. The object.

I have literally deconstructed this dead-letter email, and then reconstructed a living text: like a forensic pathologist reverse-engineering the document's corpse to infer its vitality, its animation, its communicability, its object-ivity. Here is the poem I have composed/educed/assembled/edited, an *objet de bricolage*. Read carefully, because its content-type is (as the subtitle clearly indicates) multipart/alternative.

"Diagnostic information for administrators"
(Content-Type: multipart/alternative)

You still there?

returned
Message expired, connection refused
error code error code error code
protection

LastAttemptedServerName
Original message headers

DKIM-Signature

    Message
    Accept-Language
    Content-Language

x-ms-publictraffictype: Email

TrafficTypeDiagnostic

x-exchange-antispam
   x-exchange-antispam

x-forefront

   x-forefront

received-spf: None

X-MS-Exchange-
X-MS-Exchange-
X-MS-Exchange-
X-MS-Exchange-
X-MS-Exchange-

Connection refused Socket error

None

The living email that is functioning as it should—animated, electrocharged—zings back and forth, in and out, hither and yon: too fast and complex for anyone to dissect its codes, its guts. But in death, its static detritus unfurls for any correspondent lucky enough, or stupid enough, to try to send an email to a very old friend from the very distant past: a friendship begun before email even existed. In any event, Bob and I probably have little in common any longer, nothing to email about, and the gods from the machine have probably determined that algorithmically, so *why even bother trying?* they keep asking me, in no uncertain terms.

I have saved the best for last. This is my favorite bit of the rejection message: the *pièce de résistance*, the pattern in the carpet, the secret of life, the *sine qua non*. Just nineteen lines into the NDR, this revelation sparkles. It takes me unaware. I didn't put it into my poem: it doesn't go in the poem. It is its own sublime text, free-floating, a mantra, a talisman.

```
c=relaxed/relaxed
```

Everyone is relaxed. I am relaxed. Bob is relaxed. This email is not going anywhere—relax. Be in the moment: relaxed/relaxed. (I have, seriously, integrated this epiphany into my daily mindfulness exercise.)

c = relaxed/relaxed. See equals. Relaxed, relaxed. Sea-equals relaxed. I like to see equals relaxed: if we are all equals, all the same, and we are all relaxed, relaxed, we are on the road to a happier place. Perhaps this place has bad wifi reception, minimal email connectivity. It may be in this world, or possibly beyond. If Bob and I aren't able to connect now via email, then we will catch up after we have moved on to the next stage, when we are relaxed/relaxed.

PART THREE

POSTSCRIPT

17 COMPOSE (CONT'D): HOW TO WRITE A GOOD EMAIL

Flags: useless and overly dramatic; avoid. People who use flags to highlight "important email" presuming you will take notice and respond accordingly are ridiculous. They don't get it.

Font size: 14. (Why do some people think anything over 12 is extravagantly decadent? Go to town!) Ariel, Cambria, Times Roman, you decide; Consolas, if you're in a retro mood. Colors and frou-frou graphics: distracting. Send: whenever you want, obviously, but 8:00 p.m. on Friday and 2:45 a.m. on any day will catch people's attention, and not in a good way. Salutation: go for efficiency and simplicity; this is not where you'll knock it out of the park. "Please" and "thank you": enormously underrated; easy bonus points to be had here. Sarcasm: inadvisable. Sign-off: a bit of bling is OK, but "Peace," I think, comes off as passive aggressive in these fractious times.

An "email blast" is self-evidently aggressive, tactless, scary. Never blast, and try not to get blasted yourself: don't be promiscuous with your email address (says the guy who publishes a book with his email address on the title page). Life is too short to have listservs and newsfeeds rampaging into your inbox. Cancel them, and unsubscribe to most of your other impersonal email. Opt out. Keep your eyes on the prize.

"No need to respond to this email" is a nice way to let people know that there's no need to respond to this email.

If email somehow got you in trouble, it probably won't get you out of that trouble: a more personal touch is warranted.[1]

Egocentrically, we think we are better composers than we really are: "People routinely overestimate how well they can communicate over e-mail" because it is difficult to move beyond subjective experience and imagine how others read you.[2] Acknowledge your overconfidence, your hubris. Assume that the email you are composing, like everyone else's, begins from the handicap of imperfect competence on your own part and inadequate understanding of the medium universally. Compared to natural face-to-face human conversation, email lacks body language, eye contact, and other nonverbal physiological cues like sweaty palms, flushed skin, hormonal secretions, empathetic posture, verbal tone and timbre, and so on. Emailers forget about all the vital interactive phenomena that have gone AWOL: "That's what makes email such an incendiary form of communication," writes Cary Wolfe. "All those dampening and texturing dimensions of the communication go away," and it becomes "all the more thin and brittle."[3]

Myriad books, articles, and videos claim to instruct how to write a better email, mostly from the perspectives of business protocol, institutional culture, marketing, social interaction and professional communication. All these guidebooks have dull titles—*Email Essentials*; *Send: why people email so badly and how to do it better*; *Email Legal Issues*; *Email Matters: 50 Tips to Manage Your Inbox*; *Effective Email: Concise, Clear Writing to Advance Your Business Needs*; *Communicating Effectively with Email: Courtesies, Protocols, and Time Savers*—and they live down to their dull titular promises: they are repetitive, obvious, and generally uninteresting. "Be Careful with E-Mail," a fifteen-minute video good for nothing but filling up time in a business writing class or HR orientation, warns of the "many potential pitfalls" facing the prospective emailer (e.g., your company "will know if you're downloading porn!") with a lurid moral panic that gives *Reefer Madness* a run for its money.[4]

These texts unfailingly reiterate positivistic tropes of efficiency and mannerly protocol, confronting the challenge of how to write a good email with mechanical, granular discourse analysis and business clichés. I have read through stacks of these materials and if I could save anyone else from having to do so, that alone would be worth the price of this book and the cost of my labors. They are tomes that beg to be abandoned midstream: I doubt anyone but me has read them all the way through. I like to imagine the authors of those books reading this one and blowing their minds.

The guides convey a few sensible tips, but do people really need to be told to correct misspellings and not send coworkers porn? IMHO, their raison d'être is to convey a stream of conformist anxiety. Be conventional, readers are advised: think of all the mistakes you can make in your email. Toe the line. These texts advocate and reiterate the blandness they manifest as they aim to norm the discourse. For all the problems email may have, I don't think rampant individuality is one of them.

I cannot destroy the genre of email self-help, but at least I can infuse it with more verve. Here is my own advice:

Be in a place with more plants, light, art, color, and fruit, than fluorescence, post-its, and Red Bulls. Be in a calm and engaged mood. Be excited to tell somebody something. Let your poppies grow tall.

Take a few breaths and write.

Read a draft aloud, and think about how it sounds when you recite it. (In ancient Greece, letters were always read aloud.[5]) Imagine how it might sound to the recipient reading it. Think how she will *feel* when she reads this: how you will have made her feel. Edit. Repeat.

Think about the received wisdom of the dull email primers—

change the subject line when the topic changes ❧ **Don't skip the greeting** ❧ START YOUR MESSAGE WITH A CLEAR REQUEST ❧ stay in the sweet spot when it comes to length ❧ *use third-grade language* ❧ **USE EMOTION** ❧ use rich text ❧ BE STRATEGIC ABOUT WHEN YOU SEND YOUR MESSAGE ❧ *ask for a response in your subject line* ❧ the fewer fluffy words, the more actionable the message ❧ DON'T END WITH 'CHEERS' ❧ MAKE SURE YOU ARE SENDING THE EMAIL TO THE RIGHT PERSON ❧ If there are multiple parts to the email, break it up into sections ❧ Make your subject line matter ❧ *the 'call to action' is the only thing that matters* ❧ be polite ❧ **be discreet** ❧ *sleep on it* ❧ check grammar ❧ **check spelling** ❧ CHECK PUNCTUATION ❧ USE UPPER- AND LOWER-CASE LETTERS AS APPROPRIATE ❧ Loose lips sink ships ❧ Don't address multiple people in an email request that can be answered by just one person ❧ **DON'T DEMAND A REPLY ASAP** ❧ Make things easy on the recipient ❧ One "Big Idea" per email ❧ Astonish people with your brevity ❧ Know when to pick up the phone ❧ **Stay on message** ❧ Do not use "cute" spellings ❧ mistrust autocorrect ❧ **DON'T SHOUT!!!**

and also about the limits of received wisdom.

Nuances matter. People notice nuances in writing, as we do in face-to-face interaction. While editing your writing (wearing your "grammar-hat"), also nuance your writing (using your "human-hat"). How can you tweak a word, a tone, a data point, a suggestion, to make it a little more interesting, a bit fuller, more authentic, more personable? More accessible, more sensible, more likely to be understood and affirmed? *Less bureaucratic, less organizational, less jargony*? Think of the small things people do when they're talking with each other that make a favorable impression. Good, warm, sincere eye contact; open, relaxed posture. A nice smile, or even just a hint of a smile. A warm, unpretentious handshake; a pat on the arm. Not flirtiness, but friendliness. Not obsequious, not manipulative, not calculated: just human. Get these kinds of nuances—the email equivalencies—into your writing, to convey your better self, your human charms. This is the tough part; if it were easy, *anyone* could do it.

Nuance, which will engage and delight your reader, comes with patience and sincerity. Writerly nuances are like snowflakes: idiosyncratic. The default tenor of email is dry, quick, ungenerous. Nuances are subtle, flexible, intriguing.

Be patient: a reader can sense how much time and thought the writer has taken composing an email. Most email conveys a mood of slapdash and formulaic interaction. Be on the lookout for such a tone, and disrupt it: backspace as needed, and start again . . . patiently. Write fewer emails to write better ones.

(If for some reason you want to come across in your email as a jerk—and I can't think of any reason why you would want to do this, but if you do, aim for the stars and embrace your inner dolt—simply do the opposite of everything prescribed here. Be an uptight, mechanical prig. Eschew manners and common courtesies. Shoot first and ask questions later. Periphrasis is fine.)

Consult Flaubert, or any good nineteenth-century novelist, to impress upon yourself how effective writers savor *les mots justes*. Don't actually write a Victorian email—that would be an affectation. But write a modern Victorian email. Use the right words; use good words.

Object lessons: Be honest. Be nice. Dance like no one's watching.

Don't write angry emails. Don't write an email if you're angry. Don't get in email wars. (c=relaxed/relaxed) Be keenly aware of the tawdry knee-jerk animosities and disinhibitions that are way too common in email—heckling, trolling, rudeness, bullying, sexism, racism, xenophobia, sanctimonious condescension, and a plethora of other antisocial bigotries—and simply resolve to be better than that.

Pretend that emails are more significant than they really are. Surprise your reader with your thoughtfulness, your neatness, your creativity, your sincerity, your humanity.

How we spend our days is how we spend our lives.

Writing well is the best revenge.

Probably your inbox is open behind the note you're writing, so you see a ghost of all the other dull email you have engaged with today. Tune out this stultifying milieu. Imagine it away for a few minutes. Doing that might not only help you write a better email, but also give you a nice breather. (Again: *breathe*—deeply, regularly, self-consciously: the mindfulness folks got that right. Stress and disembodiment, which *can* be alleviated, pervade the writer's psyche to the detriment of the email being composed.) Kill two birds with one stone: write a better email and have a nice moment of peace. Your brain is humming, not with officespeak and rote phrases but with thoughts about other people and things you will share with them, and wondering what they will share with you in return: mind over matter. Find the nice parts of emailing and emailing will become nicer—imagine if it got to be *something you looked forward to* in your day!

Michael Merschel, writing about his out-of-office reply being quoted in a *New York Times* article (the one about driving his daughter to college, which many people told him brought tears to their eyes), offers his own object lesson:

> When you write, everything is literature. Your grocery list. The note to your wife. The email to your mom. Your out-of-office reply. If it's going to be read by someone, you owe it to them to make it worth their time.[6]

That email will be appreciated!

¯_(ツ)_/¯

ACKNOWLEDGMENTS

I thank *Salmagundi* for permission to reprint material from an essay by Philip Stevick, "The Inner Life of E-Mail," *Salmagundi* 153/154 (Winter–Spring 2007); John Wiley and Sons for permission to reprint material from an essay by Fernando Lagraña, "E-mail and Behavioral Changes: Uses and Misuses of Electronic Communications"; and *Explorations in Media Ecology* for permission to reprint material from an essay by Joni Turville, "If e-mail could speak, what would it say? Interviewing objects in a digital world." Thanks to Jake Simonds-Malamud for providing all the technical and graphic expertise I lack. I was lucky to have the wonderful support of insanely smart editors and publishers who helped make this project come together. I am grateful to Chris Schaberg, Ian Bogost, and, at Bloomsbury, Haaris Naqvi and Amy Martin. These people's imaginative energies, packaged in Alice Marwick's brilliant cover designs, have made this series a truly monumental compendium of things that were once just things, but are now Objects that provide Lessons.

NOTES

All websites accessed August 15, 2018.

Part One

1 I render "email" unhyphenated except, as here, directly quoting sources that use the hyphen.

2 Philip Stevick, "The Inner Life of E-Mail," *Salmagundi* 153/154 (Winter–Spring 2007), 7. I thank *Salmagundi* for permission to reprint this passage.

3 Elif Batuman, *The Idiot* (New York: Penguin, 2017), 4.

4 Frances Perry, *Four American Inventors* (New York: Werner, 1901), 193.

5 Henry David Thoreau, *Walden: A Fluid-Text Edition*. Digital Thoreau. www.digitalthoreau.org/fluid-text-toc, 73a.

6 John Freeman, *The Tyranny of E-mail: The Four-Thousand-Year Journey to Your Inbox* (New York: Scribner, 2009), 15.

7 Carl Reiner and Mel Brooks, *The Complete 2000 Year Old Man* (Los Angeles: Rhino Records), 1994.

8 Tim Wu, *The Attention Merchants: The Epic Scramble to Get Inside Our Heads* (New York: Knopf, 2016), 184.

9   Scott Schnoll, *Microsoft Exchange Server 2003 Distilled* (Boston: Pearson, 2004), 4.

10 Wu, *Attention*, 184.

11 Virginia Woolf, *Jacob's Room* (New York: Harcourt, Brace, 1923), 92.

12 Simon Garfield, *To the Letter: A Celebration of the Lost Art of Letter Writing* (New York: Penguin, 2014), 426, 440.

13 Kathy Acker and McKenzie Wark, *I'm Very into You: Correspondence 1995–1996* (Cambridge: MIT Press, 2015).

14 Lydia Smith, "Final known letter written aboard Titanic fetches record £126,000 at auction." *Independent*, October 22, 2016. www.independent.co.uk/news/uk/home-news/titanic-final-letter-auction-passenger-sinking-henry-aldridge-a8013606.html.

15 Mythili Rao, "1864 Lincoln letter brings $3.4 million." CNN, April 3, 2008. www.cnn.com/2008/US/04/03/lincoln.letter/index.html.

16 Tom Wheeler, "The First Wired President." *New York Times*, May 24, 2012. opinionator.blogs.nytimes.com/2012/05/24/the-first-wired-president.

17 Angela Serratore, "Alexander Hamilton's Adultery and Apology." *Smithsonian*, July 25, 2013. www.smithsonianmag.com/history/alexander-hamiltons-adultery-and-apology-180 21947.

18 "Is There a Santa Claus?" *New York Sun*, September 21, 1897. www.nysun.com/editorials/yes-virginia/68502.

19 Annalisa Merelli, "I know John Podesta has had a rough couple of days—but he is wrong about risotto, and someone needs to tell America," *Quartz*, October 12, 2016. qz.com/807952/wikileaks-emails-reveal-clinton-campaign-chief-john-podesta-is-wrong-about-risotto.

20   Freeman, *Tyranny*, 51.

21   Dave Malloy, *Natasha, Pierre & the Great Comet of 1812*
(2012), "Letters." www.genius.com/Dave-malloy-letters-lyrics.

Part Two

1   Fernando Lagraña, *E-mail and Behavioral Changes: Uses
and Misuses of Electronic Communications* (London: Wiley,
2016), 3.1.

2   Joni Turville, "If E-mail Could Speak, What Would It Say?
Interviewing Objects in a Digital World." *Explorations in
Media Ecology* 16.2/3 (2017): 157.

Chapter 1

1   Merlin Mann, "Inbox Zero," Google Tech Talks, July 23, 2007.
www.youtube.com/watch?v=z9UjeTMb3Yk 10:30.

2   Stanley Solomon, "Corresponding effects: Artless writing
in the age of E-mail." *Modern Age* 40.3 (Summer 1998):
319–24.

3   Emma Rooksby, *Email and Ethics: Style and Ethical Relations
in Computer-Mediated Communication* (London: Routledge,
2002), 4–5.

4   Annie Dillard, *The Writing Life* (New York: Harper, 1989), 32.

5   Mahatma Gandhi, *Non-Violence in Peace and War* (Navajivan:
Ahmedabad, 1948), 1: 339.

6 Adrienne LaFrance, "The Triumph of Email," *Atlantic*, January 6, 2016. www.theatlantic.com/technology/archive/2016/01/what-comes-after-email/422625.

7 Harry Watt and Basil Wright, dirs., *Night Mail* (UK: Associated British Film Distributors, 1936).

8 William Caxton, *Oxford English Dictionary* usage quotation for "letter," n. 1, 5.a.

9 Monty Python, "Spam." genius.com/Monty-python-spam-song-lyrics.

10 "Series of Tubes," *Wikipedia*. en.wikipedia.org/wiki/Series_of_tubes.

11 Wheeler, "Wired."

12 Peter Manseau, "How We Find Our Way to the Dead." *New York Times*, October 28, 2017. www.nytimes.com/2017/10/28/opinion/sunday/death-ghosts-culture.html.

13 Peter Robinson, "A New Email App Lets You Mess with Loved Ones from Beyond the Grave," *Vice*, July 6, 2016. www.vice.com/en_us/article/zn8e9w/phoenix-the-service-that-lets-you-email-people-after-you-die.

14 Alan Gardiner, *Egyptian Grammar, Being an Introduction to the Study of Hieroglyphs* (Oxford: Griffith Institute, Ashmolean Museum, 1957), 445.

15 E. E. Cummings, *100 Selected Poems* (New York: Grove, 1954), 84.

16 Garfield, *Letter*, 395.

17 Wu, *Attention*, 184–85.

18 "Email pioneer Ray Tomlinson dead at 74." *Sydney Morning Herald*, March 6, 2016. www.smh.com.au/technology/web-culture/email-pioneer-ray-tomlinson-dead-at-74-20160306-gnbspq.html.

19 Freeman, *Tyranny*, 58.

20 Rooksby, *Ethics*, 2.

21 "Mail," *Oxford English Dictionary*.

22 Donald Knuth, Stanford University webpage. www-cs-faculty. stanford.edu/~knuth/email.html.

23 https://twitter.com/ibogost/status/917504870424424449

Chapter 2

1 Molly Wood, "How to Keep Data Out of Hackers' Hands." *New York Times*, August 6, 2014. www.nytimes.com/interacti ve/2014/08/05/technology/what-you-need-to-know-with-rus sian-hack.html.

2 Martin Paul Eve, *Password* (New York: Bloomsbury, 2016).

3 "Password," *Oxford English Dictionary*.

4 Ibid.

5 Ibid., usage examples.

6 Norman McLeod, dir., *Horse Feathers* (U.S.: Paramount, 1932).

Chapter 3

1 William Shakespeare, *Troilus and Cressida*, act 1, scene 3.

2 Martin Amis, *The Information* (New York: Vintage, 1995), 338.

3 John Pavlus, "How Email Became the Most Reviled Communication Experience Ever," *Fastcodesign*, June 15, 2015.

www.fastcodesign.com/3047273/how-email-became-the-most-reviled-communication-experience-ever.

4 Ibid.

5 Ibid.

6 Alexis Madrigal, "Email Is Still the Best Thing on the Internet." *Atlantic*, August 14, 2014. www.theatlantic.com/technology/archive/2014/08/why-e-mail-will-never-die/375973.

7 Finn Brunton, *Spam: A Shadow History of the Internet* (Cambridge: MIT Press, 2013), 204.

Chapter 5

1 Solomon, "Corresponding," 319.

2 Ibid., 321.

3 Radicati Group, "Email Statistics Report, 2017–2021." www.radicati.com/wp/wp-content/uploads/2017/01/Email-Statistics-Report-2017-2021-Executive-Summary.pdf.

4 "Internet live stats," www.internetlivestats.com/one-second/#email-band.

5 "The Infinite Monkey Theorem," expounded in Émile Borel's 1913 essay "Mécanique Statistique et Irréversibilité," circulates widely: for example, in Jorge Luis Borges' 1939 story "The Total Library": "a halfdozen monkeys provided with typewriters would, in a few eternities, produce all the books in the British Museum."

6 Guy Bleus, "The Mothers of Internet," Mail-Art Networking Archives, 1999.

7   *E-Pêle-Mêle* 3.1 (December 1997), Electronic Mail Art Netzine, ed. Guy Bleus.

8   Elsa Philippe, interview. *Streaming Festival*, 2012. www.stream ingfestival.com/video/interview.php?ai=1598

9   Elsa Philippe, *I am you all*, 2018. https://mailchi.mp/screen-space/elsa-is-you-all.

10 Museum of Email & Digital Communications. email-museum.com/about/.

11 Batuman, *Idiot*, 3.

12 Ibid., 4.

13 Christian Lorentzen, "Elif Batuman on Writer's Block, the Shame of Youth, and *The Idiot*, Her Great Novel About the Magical Early Age of Email," *Vulture*, March 10, 2017. www.vulture.com/2017/03/elif-batuman-on-writers-block-and-th e-magic-of-early-email.html.

14 Adaobi Tricia Nwaubani, *I Do Not Come to You by Chance* (New York: Hyperion, 2009), 178.

15 Britney Spears, "E-Mail My Heart," 1999. genius.com/Brit ney-spears-e-mail-my-heart-lyrics

16 Julia Wayne, "Britney Spears Teaches Us About Funky, Cool Emails in Throwback Thursday Video." *Wetpaint*, February 6, 2014. www.wetpaint.com/britney-spears-funky-cool-emails-801941.

17 Jordan Bassett, "Remembering Britney Spears' Weirdest Song: 'E-Mail My Heart.'" *NME*, September 28, 2016. www.nme.com/blogs/nme-blogs/britney-spears-weirdest-song-ever-759 850#b5WpXXysSmx4HAqp.99.

18 Kristie Rohwedder, "Britney Spears' 'E-mail My Heart' Is As Heartwarming As The Sound Of AOL Dialing Up." *Bustle*, June 23, 2015. www.bustle.com/articles/92478-britney-spears-e-mail-my-heart-is-as-heartwarming-as-the-sound-of-aol-dialing-up.

19 Maitri Mehta, "6 of Britney Spears' Weirdest Lyrics & Yes, 'Email My Heart' Definitely Makes The Cut." *Bustle*, August 21, 2015. www.bustle.com/articles/105606-6-of-britney-spears-weirdest-lyrics-yes-email-my-heart-definitely-makes-the-cut.

20 All lyrics from genius.com.

21 Stevick, "Inner," 8.

22 David Li, "Here's what the 'You've Got Mail' guy is up to now." *New York Post*, November 7, 2016. nypost.com/2016/11/07/the-youve-got-mail-guy-is-doing-this-now.

23 Nora Ephron, dir., *You've Got Mail* (U.S.: Warner Brothers, 1998).

24 Kathy Acker and McKenzie Wark, *Into You*, 14.

25 "If only they had email in 1810," www.lostopinions.com/austen/email.

26 Kathryn Doyle, "Shakespeare's Work Emails," *McSweeney's*, October 29, 2014. www.mcsweeneys.net/articles/shakespeares-work-emails.

Chapter 7

1 Watt and Wright, *Night Mail*.

2 "Snail Mail," *Wikipedia*,. en.wikipedia.org/wiki/Snail_mail.

3 "Snail Mail," *Urban Dictionary*. www.urbandictionary.com/define.php?term=snail%20mail.

4 William Shakespeare, *1 Henry IV* act 2, scene 4.

5 Psalms 144:6.

6 Exodus 9:14.

7 Stephen Sondheim, *A Little Night Music*, 1973.

8 Garfield, *Letter*, 22.

Chapter 8

1 Freeman, *Tyranny*, 103.

2 Stanley Kubrick, dir., *Dr. Strangelove or: How I Learned to Stop Worrying and Love the Bomb* (U.S.: Columbia, 1964).

3 Workfront, "U.S. State of Enterprise Work Report 2016–2017." www.workfront.com/resources/2016-17-u-s-state-of-marketing-work-report.

4 Cory Doctorow, "Writing in the Age of Distraction." *Locus*, January 7, 2009. www.locusmag.com/Features/2009/01/cory-doctorow-writing-in-age-of.html.

5 Jonah Lehrer, "Our Cluttered Minds." *New York Times*, June 3, 2010, BR22.

6 Ron Friedman, "The Cost of Continuously Checking Email," *Harvard Business Review*, July 4, 2014. hbr.org/2014/07/the-cost-of-continuously-checking-email.

7 Cal Newport, *Deep Work: Rules for Focused Success in a Distracted World* (NY: Grand Central, 2016), 6.

8 Freeman, *Tyranny*, 8–9.

9 Claudia Dreifus, "Why We Can't Look Away From Our Screens." *New York Times*, March 6, 2017. www.nytimes.com/2017/03/06/science/technology-addiction-irresistible-by-adam-alter.html.

10 "Analog shit," *Urban Dictionary*. www.urbandictionary.com/define.php?term=Analog%20shit.

11 Mann, "Inbox Zero," 3:00-5:00.

12 Ibid.

13 Ibid., 14:00.

14 Ibid., 32:00.

15 Bourree Lam, "After-Work Email," *Atlantic*, April 26, 2015. www.theatlantic.com/business/archive/2015/04/the-after-work-email-quandary/391313.

Chapter 9

1 "Blind carbon copy," *Wikipedia*. en.wikipedia.org/wiki/Blind_carbon_copy.

Chapter 10

1 Abigail Sellen and Richard Harper, *The Myth of the Paperless Office* (Cambridge: MIT Press, 2001), 13.

2 Max Smolaks, "Number of data centers to decrease after 2017." *Data Center Dynamics*, November 12, 2014. www.datacenterdynamics.com/content-tracks/colo-cloud/number-of-data-centers-to-decrease-after-2017/91495.fullarticle.

Chapter 11

1 David Shipley and Will Schwalbe, *Send* (New York: Knopf, 2007), 27.

Chapter 12

1   Emily Gould, "The Art of the Out-of-Office Reply." *New York Times*, August 27, 2015. www.nytimes.com/2015/08/28/fashion/the-art-of-the-out-of-office-reply.html. Replies from Dan Kois, Mallory Ortberg, Michael Merschel.

2   Avery Blank, "What Successful People Say in Out of Office Email." *Forbes*, January 25, 2017. www.forbes.com/sites/averyblank/2017/01/25/what-successful-people-say-in-out-of-office-email-that-youre-missing-out-on.

Chapter 13

1   Mihir Patkar, "4 Influential People Who Don't Use Email, and Why," *Makeuseof*, July 7, 2015. www.makeuseof.com/tag/4-influential-people-dont-use-email.

2   Ibid.

3   Colin Campbell, "John McCain's explanation for why he doesn't use email is absolute gold," *Business Insider*, March 4, 2015. www.businessinsider.com/john-mccains-explanation-for-why-he-doesnt-use-email-2015-3.

4   Associated Press, "Kagan: Court hasn't 'gotten to' email," *Politico*, August 20, 2013. www.politico.com/story/2013/08/kagan-supreme-court-email-095724.

5   Eliot Spitzer, "Cleaning Up Capitalism," *Fast Company*, January 1, 1995.

6   Anthony Haden-Guest, "Of Eco and E-mail," *New Yorker*, June 26, 1995, 58.

7   Libby Brooks, "Email? Who needs it?" *Guardian*, July 18, 2003. www.theguardian.com/g2/story/0,3604,1000434,00.html.

8   Meghan Keneally, "Donald Trump Is No 'Email Person' but 'Knows Things About Hacking,'" *ABCNews*, January 2, 2017. abcnews.go.com/Politics/donald-trump-email-person-things-hacking/story?id=44511376.

9   Associated Press, "Trump Says he Doesn't Trust Computers as He Rings in 2017," *Fortune*, January 1, 2017. www.fortune.com/2017/01/01/trump-doesnt-trust-computers.

10   Knuth, Stanford.

11   Patkar, "Influential."

12   Alissa Rubin, "France Lets Workers Turn Off, Tune Out and Live Life," *New York Times*, January 2, 2017. www.nytimes.com/2017/01/02/world/europe/france-work-email.html.

13   Lam, "After-Work."

14   Andrew Martin and Anne Curzan, "What Happened When the Dean's Office Stopped Sending Emails After-Hours," *Chronicle of Higher Education*, April 12, 2018. www.chronicle.com/article/What-Happened-When-the/243082.

15   Hillary Rodham Clinton, *What Happened* (New York: Simon & Schuster, 2017), 292–93.

Chapter 14

1   Donald Trump, Trump Twitter Archive, June 21, 2016, June 30, 2016, July 13, 2016. www.trumptwitterarchive.com/archive.

2   Dan Merica, "Clinton: 'If the election had been on October 27, I would be your president,'" May 2, 2017. www.cnn.co m/2017/05/02/politics/hillary-clinton-planned-parenthood-women-for-women/index.html.

3   Eugene Kiely, "Trump, Pence 'Acid Wash' Facts," September 8, 2016. www.factcheck.org/2016/09/trump-pence-acid-wash-facts.

4   Nina Burleigh, "The George W. Bush White House 'Lost' 22 Million Emails," September 12, 2016. www.newsweek.co m/2016/09/23/george-w-bush-white-house-lost-22-million-emails-497373.html.

5   National Archives, "National Archives Announces a New Model for the Preservation and Accessibility of Presidential Records," May 3, 2017. www.archives.gov/press/press-releas es/2017/nr17-54.

6   Ashley Parker, "Donald Trump Calls on Russia to Find Hillary Clinton's Missing Emails," July 27, 2016. www.nytimes. com/2016/07/28/us/politics/donald-trump-russia-clinton-emails.html.

7   Greg Walters, "The Russians Hacked Hillary Clinton and the DNC on the Very Day Trump Asked Them To," July 13, 2018. news.vice.com/en_us/article/pawbg7/russians-hacked-hillary-clinton-and-the-dnc-on-the-very-day-trump-asked-them-to-according-to-mueller-investigation.

8   Clinton, *What Happened,* 292.

9   Ibid., 292–93.

10 "Hillary Clinton Email Archive," March 16, 2016. wikileaks. org/clinton-emails.

11 Lily Newman, "Actually, Clinton Should Have Destroyed Her Phones Better," September 7, 2016. www.wired.com/2016/09/actually-clinton-destroyed-phones-better.

12 Clinton, *What Happened*, 291.

13 Ibid., 291–92.

14 Brian Barrett, "The FBI Has Clinton's Email Server. Now What?" August 20, 2015. www.wired.com/2015/08/clinton-email-server-wipe.

Chapter 16

1 Common 503 errors, *Fastly*. docs.fastly.com/guides/debugging/common-503-errors.html.

2 "Guru Meditation," *Wikipedia*. www.wikipedia.org/wiki/Guru_Meditation.

3 All lyrics from genius.com.

Part Three

Chapter 17

1 Shipley and Schwalbe, *Send*, 173.

2 Justin Kruger, Nicholas Epley, and Zhi-Wen Ng, "Egocentrism Over E-Mail: Can We Communicate as Well as We Think?" *Journal of Personality and Social Psychology* 89.6 (2005): 925–36.

3 Cary Wolfe, "Is Humanism Really Humane?" *New York Times*, January 9, 2017. www.nytimes.com/2017/01/09/opinion/is-humanism-really-humane.html.

4 Films Media Group, "Be Careful with E-Mail," Video Education Australasia, Bendigo, 2001.

5 Garfield, *Letter*, 48.

6 Michael Merschel, "How my out-of-office reply became national news, and what we can learn from that." *Dallas Morning News*, August 3, 2016. www.dallasnews.com/arts/books/2016/08/03/ office-reply-became-national-news-can-learn.

INDEX